D0610027

HOW TO RAISE AN
AMAZING CHILD
THE MONTESSORI WAY

Staffordshire

3 8014 11083 4022

HOW TO RAISE AN
AMAZING CHILD
THE MONTESSORI WAY

TIM SELDIN
PRESIDENT OF THE
MONTESSORI FOUNDATION

contents

introduction

I can't remember a time when I wasn't involved in the world of Montessori – for me it is a way of life.

This book is a compilation of my personal experience as a young child, as a father, as a Montessori guide, and as something of a coach to many families who have sought a better way to raise their children in a spirit of kindness, partnership, and respect. Much of what I have learned came from observing and listening to my children, and from my mistakes.

Being a parent is a full-time job. Once upon a time, raising a family seemed straightforward. Mums stayed at home and looked after the children, while dads went out to work. Children were generally obedient, if only because their parents kept a tight rein on their activities and punished them severely if they went astray.

Today, there are all sorts of families – single working mums, stay-at-home dads, families where children have two mums or two dads, and families with three or more generations living together. In many families, a parent is not at home all day; both parents may have a career or business, or they may have to work just to make ends meet.

Young children may be cared for by a parent or grandparent, a nanny or babysitter at home, by a childminder, or in a nursery.

In many countries, divorce is common. Many parents juggle the responsibilities of work and parenting in a single-parent household, or co-parent in separate households while trying to provide stability and consistency for their children.

Meanwhile, we are given constant reminders on the internet, on television, and in the media that the right environment and experiences are crucially important for infants, toddlers, and young children. We learn that children's brains are programmed to learn, but only if they are stimulated at an early age. As if we did not have enough guilt before, now we worry about whether we are good enough as early childhood parent-educators.

Most of us long to give our children the best home environment that we possibly can, within the limits of our time and resources. It is also true that every parent is a teacher. The mission that

"Most of us long to give our children the best home environment that we possibly can."

we have undertaken is not simply to feed, cuddle, and protect our children. We also need to teach them to become independent, self-confident, successful adults, who are happy and fulfilled in their lives. While that journey takes many years, it helps to have some idea of where you are heading and why we do what we do along the way.

If you have a young child and are eager for a fresh perspective and some practical suggestions, then this book is for you. It is filled not only with ideas for activities to do together, but with a message that life can be celebrated. The small everyday things that we can do to mark special occasions and to reaffirm our love for one another can make all the difference in the world, both for your child and for your own life as a mum or dad.

Tim Seldin
President, The Montessori Foundation

1
why Montessori?

the highs and lows of parenting

Children are one of life's greatest gifts – but raising caring, happy children in this modern world can be a challenge to any parent.

Our connection with our children is formed before birth, and lasts for our entire lives. Over the years, we are there beside them as they learn to smile, crawl, speak their first words, take their first steps, and together we mark the milestones in their journey towards adulthood.

Life with children is not always easy. Along with the hugs and cuddles, we share their sleepless nights, the times when they are ill, their temper tantrums and fights with siblings, and the many other challenges of being a parent. As they get older it seems that our children come to know us better than we know ourselves. They learn what buttons to push to make us aggravated and how they can best manipulate us into giving in over something that they want. There are times when we wish our children came with a parenting manual.

It is not unusual for parents to be unsure about how to raise nice kids in this modern world. All around, our children see and hear other children answering back to their parents, arguing in the playground, and saying unkind things to one

Connected for life
From birth our children become the focus of our love and attention, forming a bond that carries through to adulthood.

another. Parenting advice abounds, but much of it doesn't seem to work that well. This is in part because it tends to offer a cookbook approach with detailed suggestions about what to do in specific situations, rather than a comprehensive, systematic approach to parenting.

A different approach

My life has been touched deeply by the work of a brilliant woman: Maria Montessori. As a child, I went to a wonderful school that was inspired by her work and as an adult I have had the privilege to teach in and later lead that same school for 25 years. Her message and the insights and practical strategies that she taught have influenced hundreds of thousands, if not millions, of parents and children around the world. The Montessori approach is best known in the schools that bear her name, but it is equally useful and easy to adopt in your own home.

Montessori's principles for working with children are based on a holistic approach that begins at birth (or as young as possible) and builds over the years as children become more mature. Understood correctly, it has the advantage of working very well with a wide range of children. It is an entire system that has been tested over the past 100 years and can be implemented as a whole or in part. Try it – you should find that it works for you too.

To do this, you don't need to become a Montessori teacher, nor is there a need to create a Montessori school in your home. But by implementing as many of the suggestions in this book as you can into your home and your family's life, I believe that you will find yourself becoming more effective as a parent, and more able to build a home filled with warmth, love, kindness and respect.

Testing limits
As children begin to demonstrate their drive for independence, the challenges of parenthood become more apparent.

what is
Montessori?

One hundred years ago a young Italian woman devised a new approach to education based on a foundation of encouragement and respect.

Maria Montessori was born in 1870 in Italy, a country that at that time was especially conservative in its attitude towards women. Despite many obstacles, Montessori was the first Italian woman to become a doctor. She went on to teach at the medical school of the University of Rome, and, through its free clinics, came into frequent contact with the children of the poor. Through her work she became convinced that each and every child is born with an amazing human potential, which can develop only if adults provide children with the right stimulation during the first few years of life.

Anxious to prove her point, in 1907 Montessori started to oversee a nursery for working-class children who were too young to go to school. Located in one of Rome's worst slums, this became her first Casa dei Bambini or "children's house". Growing up with little attention and in appalling conditions, many of the children who entered were aggressive, impatient, and disorderly.

Montessori began her work by teaching the older children how to help out with everyday tasks. To her amazement, three and four year olds took great delight in learning practical living skills. Soon these children were taking care of the school, assisting with the preparation and serving of meals and helping to maintain a spotless environment. Their behaviour changed from that of street urchins running wild to models of grace and courtesy.

> "Montessori's work lives on today. Her systematic approach can be replicated and sustained in almost any situation."

A child's world

Montessori recognized that little children experience a sense of frustration in an adult-sized world, so she had miniature jugs and bowls prepared and found knives that fitted into a child's tiny hand. She had carpenters build child-sized tables and chairs that were light enough for children to move without adult help. The children loved to sit on the floor, so she gave them little rugs to define their work areas and they quickly learned to walk carefully around the rugs rather than disrupt each other's work.

After spending countless hours observing and interacting with children, Montessori concluded that they pass through a number of distinct developmental stages (see pages 14–17), each one being characterized by specific inclinations, interests, and ways of thinking. She found that children have their own logic at each stage of development, along with certain preferred activities and natural tendencies in behaviour.

She observed how children respond to a calm and orderly environment in which everything has its allocated place. She watched the children learn to control their movements, and noted their dislike of the way the calm was disturbed when they stumbled or dropped something. She gave them the opportunity to develop their sense of independence and recognized their increasing levels of self-respect and confidence as they were taught and encouraged to do things for themselves.

A new beginning
Maria Montessori took a scientific approach to education, developing equipment and observing children as they worked with it.

International appeal

The first children's house received instant acclaim and interest surged around the world. As an internationally respected scientist, Montessori had a rare credibility and she captured the interest of national leaders and scientists, labour leaders and factory owners, teachers and mothers. She gave up her medical practice to devote her energy to overseeing the spread of Montessori schools around the world. A tireless advocate for the rights and intellectual potential of all children, she continued to develop programmes such as "Education and Peace" until her death in 1952. Montessori's work lives on today. Her systematic approach can be replicated and sustained in almost any situation. Some people are attracted to the calm, responsible behaviour shown by these students, and appreciate their love for learning. Others applaud the freedom, spontaneity, and independence that Montessori gives young children.

sensitive periods
for learning

Children pass through "sensitive periods" in which they are primed to learn, and some of these opportunities don't come twice.

Montessori recognized that children go through stages of intellectual interest and curiosity – which she called "sensitive periods" – in which they become intrigued and absorbed by particular aspects of their environment. It is important that we understand this process because each stage represents an opportunity which, if taken advantage of, can profoundly influence our children's development.

Montessori identified several different sensitive periods occurring from birth through to age six (see pages 16–17). Each one refers to a predisposition

for children to acquire specific characteristics. A sensitive period is a kind of compulsion, motivating young children to focus intently on some particular aspect of their environment, day after day, without becoming tired or bored. For example, during the first few years of life, children are in a sensitive period for language. They pay close attention to what we say and how we say it, and, before we know it, they speak the same language as us and with a similar accent. Clearly, this is a biological mechanism, hard-wired into children, that helps them to develop skills and talents that are inherently part of our heritage as human beings.

> "During a sensitive period children become intrigued by an aspect of their environment."

Learning foundation

Inevitably, the beginning and end of each sensitive period will differ from child to child, so we need to watch carefully and respond to our children individually. Remember that your child's learning during these early stages is the foundation upon which much that follows will be built. When parents and teachers recognize and take advantage of the sensitive periods through which children pass, they can become more effective in supporting their learning and development.

Limited opportunity

During a sensitive period, children can learn new things, master new skills, or develop aspects of their brain's abilities almost unconsciously. However, sensitive periods are transitory states. Once children have mastered the skill or concept in which they were absorbed, the sensitive period seems to disappear, so if children are not exposed to the right experience and stimulation at the right time, the opportunity to learned will pass. The skills can still be learned, but it may require years of hard work and drill. This is why, for example, learning one or more languages is relatively easy for children at the age of two and three when they are in a sensitive period for language, but much more difficult for most of us as adults.

YOUR CHILD'S
BRAIN

Scientists have shown that experiences during sensitive periods of development change the circuitry of the brain. Patterns of connections are made that become part of the brain's "stable landscape" – which is the foundation for future learning and behaviour.

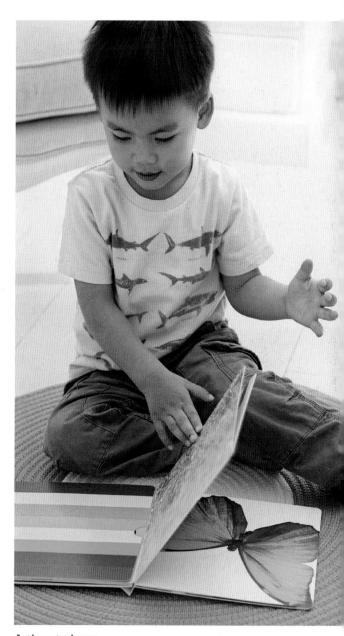

A time to learn
Given the right stimulation at the right time, children are able to learn almost unconsciously.

IN PRACTICE Sensitive periods (birth to six years)

These sensitive stages are sometimes called "periods of power". Montessori believed that they should be encouraged, not just for cognitive development, but also for a child's happiness.

**Movement
birth to one year**
Your baby's random movements become coordinated and controlled as he learns to grasp, touch, turn, balance, crawl, and walk.

**Language
birth to six years**
Starting with practice coos and sounds, your baby progresses from babble to words, phrases, then sentences.

**Order
six months to four years**
This stage is characterized by your child's love of routines and a desire for consistency and repetition. Everything must have its place.

**Small objects
one to four years**
Your child will adore handling small objects and noticing tiny details as hand–eye coordination becomes increasingly refined.

**Toilet training
18 months to three years**
As her nervous system becomes better developed and integrated, your child will become able to gain control of her bladder and bowels.

**Music
two to six years**
When music is part of his everyday life, your child will show spontaneous interest in the development of pitch, rhythm, and melody.

Grace and courtesy
two to six years
Your child will love to imitate polite and considerate behaviour leading to an internalization of these qualities into her personality.

Senses
two to six years
Sensory education begins at birth, but from two your child will be absorbed by sensorial experiences (sights, sounds, tactile sensations, tastes, and scents).

Writing
three to four years
Montessori discovered that writing precedes reading and begins with attempts to reproduce letters and numbers with a pencil and paper.

Reading
three to five years
Children show a spontaneous interest in symbols and the sounds they represent – soon they are sounding out words.

Spatial relationships
four to six years
As children develop an understanding of spatial relationships, they begin to work out complex puzzles.

Mathematics
four to six years
Montessori found ways to give children a concrete experience of maths in the period of sensitivity for numbers and quantities.

how a child's
brain develops

During the first six years, children's brains are developing at a much faster pace than at any other time in childhood and adolescence.

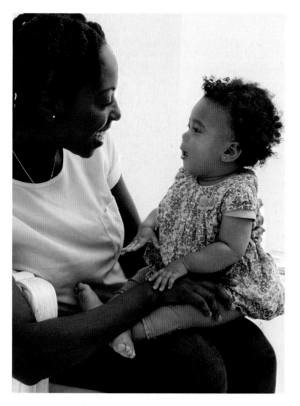

Today there is widespread agreement among scientists that, from birth, a child's brain develops in predictable ways that are incredibly responsive to their environment. The brain is pre-wired to acquire skills such as language, but all of its growth and changes are brought about by external stimulation. Whatever children are exposed to at home and in group settings during these critical early years lays the foundation for everything that will follow.

Maria Montessori documented the way children develop by carefully observing children from birth to six years. More than 100 years later, her conclusions are confirmed by new techniques in brain research with young children. MRI scanning reveals the hidden evidence of how the developing brain responds to intellectual and sensory stimulation

Happy talk
Motherese describes the sing-song speech mothers use naturally with babies. Science has shown that these are the tones babies hear best.

by laying down neural pathways and building complex and enduring networks. During these years, children will learn naturally, given the right environment, encouragement, and opportunities.

The science of nurture

What do children really need aside from good nutrition and good sleep during their first six years of life? Here is what research tells us.

• Intellectual, emotional, and social development are interconnected. Brain development is optimized when children feel loved, safe, and secure. Cuddling and comforting lays foundations that help children to deal with stress in later life.

• Sensory experiences using sight, hearing, touch, taste, smell, and movement stimulate nerve cells, which are present in the brain from birth, to spark together and build permanent connections.

• Montessori suggested that the brain was "hand-made" through children exploring and manipulating things in their environment. Science bears this out: physical activity boosts the production of cells in the hippocampus, a part of the brain with a key role in memory and learning.

• The size of a child's vocabulary is a key predictor of success in school. From birth, babies are learning the sounds of their own language. Talking, reading, and singing together enriches their vocabulary.

• The brain develops in predictable ways, but each brain and each child is unique. Every child needs parents who will watch for his cues, rhythms, and moods and respond to them appropriately.

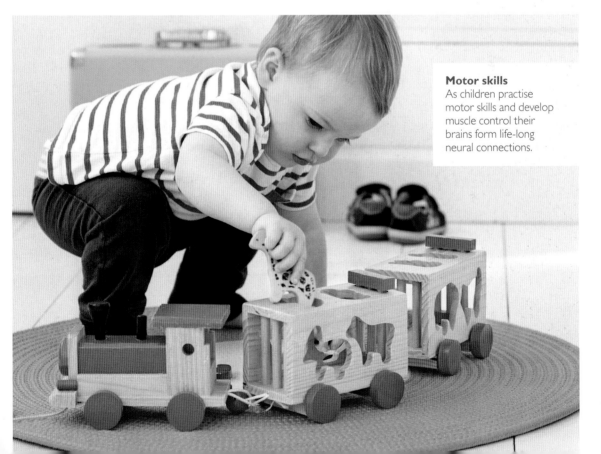

Motor skills
As children practise motor skills and develop muscle control their brains form life-long neural connections.

the magic of Montessori schools

The Montessori message is just as meaningful today and is thriving in schools around the world.

Children who are treated with respect and who are encouraged to try new skills learn more readily to do things for themselves. Montessori taught that a child who feels respected and competent will develop a far greater level of emotional well-being than a child who is simply loved and doted upon.

Montessori teachers share a conviction that success in school is directly tied to the degree to which children believe they are capable, independent human beings. Young children are shown how to pour liquids, write letters, and compute sums. Older children are shown research techniques, internet search skills, and more advanced forms of writing and maths. When children develop a meaningful degree of independence, they set a pattern for a lifetime of good work habits, self-discipline, and a sense of responsibility.

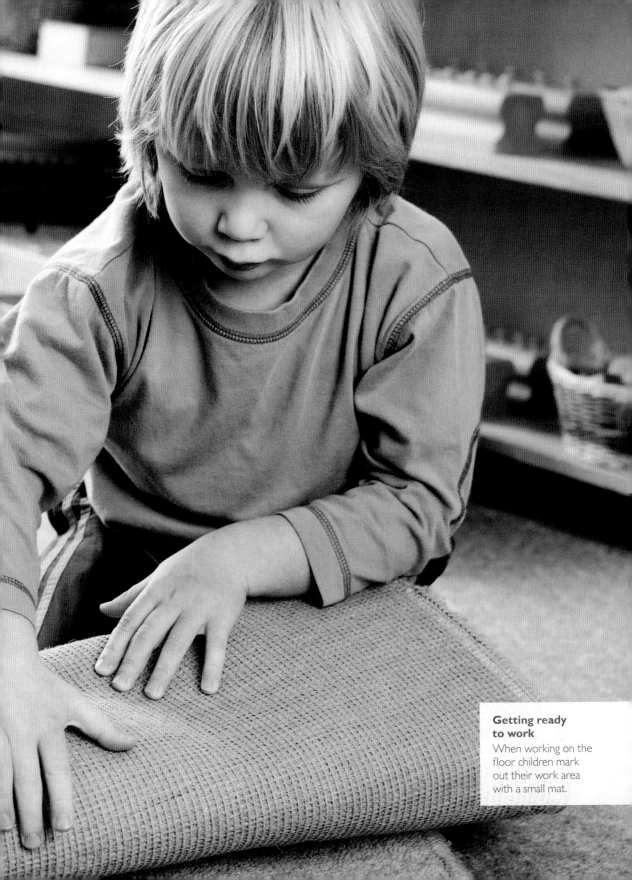

Getting ready to work

When working on the floor children mark out their work area with a small mat.

Freedom to learn

In a Montessori classroom there are some basic ground rules about behaviour and tidiness, but beyond these, children are free to choose whatever activity they wish and to work with it for as long as they want to. They are free to move about and work alone or with others at will. Much of the time children select work that captures their interest, although teachers help them to choose activities that will present new challenges and new areas of inquiry. When they are finished with an activity, children are expected to put the materials back where they belong. Students are taught to manage their own community, and they develop independence and strong leadership skills.

Such guidelines easily adapt to the home environment. If you create a welcoming but orderly space for your children and allow them to work and play freely, their confidence and independence will blossom.

Neat and tidy
The Montessori classroom creates a sense of order that encourages children to become self-disciplined and independent.

IN PRACTICE Tailor-made activities

The equipment in Montessori schools is attractive, the right size for small hands, and designed as a complete task, so children have the satisfaction of seeing the results of their work.

Buttoning up
Practising on a dressing frame helps children master the skills needed to dress themselves.

Shoe polishing
Children love to polish small brass and silver objects, then move on to polishing their own shoes.

Learning to pour
Small china or glass jugs, just right for children's hands, are used to teach them how to pour carefully.

Learning letters
Children learn to read phonetically. They compose words and sentences using a "Movable Alphabet" made up of blue vowels and pink consonants.

Handwriting
To help develop the hand–eye control needed to grasp and write with a pencil, children trace shapes onto paper using metal stencils.

Sensorial equipment
Children develop their visual discrimination of size as they slot wooden cylinders, graded in size and depth, into holes in the block.

right from
the beginning

Babies are born curious, creative, and intelligent. Alongside basic baby care, enrich your child's world to help him achieve his full potential.

While babies are different from adults in many important ways, each is a full and complete human being who is present in the room with us, absorbing every sight, sound, smell, and touch that he experiences into his deepest memories. When, as parents, we truly understand this, we can become more aware of the impression left by what we do, what we say, and what we allow our children to come into contact with from the moment of their birth and through the first days, months, and years of their lives.

A gentle birth

There was a time, not so many years ago, when babies were delivered in hospital operating rooms. After nine months floating in the warm, cosy, dark

Absorbent minds
From the moment they are born, children are responsive and receptive to all aspects of their environment.

environment of their mother's womb, experiencing only muffled sounds, babies went through the trauma of birth and entered a brightly lit, noisy room where the air was cool, and where they were handled roughly. It seems difficult now to imagine a newborn being held by a leg as the doctor gave it a swat on its bottom to get it breathing, yet this used to be common practice. Next, rather than allowing mother and baby to meet one another and rest, the umbilical cord was swiftly cut and the baby was taken off into another room to be weighed and washed.

Today, thanks in part to Montessori's influence, more compassionate health care professionals assist in the process of birth. Modern birthing centres and hospitals use subdued lighting; the room temperature is kept warm, soothing music can be played and everyone speaks in hushed voices. After the birth, the newborn is placed on the mother's tummy to rest and bond before being washed off, weighed, and checked over. Of course, these practices are unlikely to be followed in emergencies, and when babies are born by C-section in an operating theatre, but care after the birth should be relaxed and calm.

"Babies are full and complete human beings…absorbing every sight, sound, smell, and touch that they experience."

A wonderful journey
Every physical milestone your baby achieves is driven by the need to experience more.

Bonding with your newborn

In the first few hours after birth, there is a sensitive period in which infants form a particularly close bond with their parents. According to Dr Silvana Montanaro, from the Association Montessori Internationale (AMI) Assistants to Infancy centre in Rome, "Research has shown that the extent and quality of care the mother provides the child are strongly conditioned by the way they spend their time together during the first days after birth."

This connection begins from the physical contact experienced as the baby is cuddled and touched by his parents, and soon becomes the emotional bond that we celebrate in all healthy relationships between parents and children. It is a two-way connection. The baby feels safe in his parents' arms, and forms a powerful and lasting impression of their faces, smells, and the sound of their voices; at the same time, the parents usually fall head over heels in love with their child, which goes a long way to helping them keep going in the early months when they are deprived of sleep and adjusting to new parenthood.

Both parents should take turns holding and caressing their newborn to ensure a close bond is formed with each of them. Gently stroke your baby while he lies in your lap or hold him against your bare chest to establish the warmth and closeness of skin-to-skin contact.

Almost all babies, and in particular those who are born prematurely or who face medical challenges, respond beautifully to gentle infant massage. Massage relaxes your baby and at the same time deepens the bonding process. It is also known to contribute to restful sleep and good digestion. There are many books and videos available that demonstrate massage techniques and explain the benefits of massaging your baby.

Soothing and settling

Babies enjoy the sounds of baby talk from adults: cooing, singing, and talking in silly voices all tend to hold their attention. And, of course, it is universally acknowledged that reciting poetry or nursery rhymes, singing lullabies, or reading aloud as you gently rock in a chair are the best ways to soothe a crying baby.

Some babies startle and cry easily, while others find it difficult to fall asleep or they may be unusually sensitive to touch, light, or sound. Don't be alarmed if your baby reacts in this way or if he appears to turn away when you speak or sing to him. Just keep working at your bond – touch your baby gently, speak to him softly, try to keep noise levels down around him, and keep the lighting fairly low. In time, he will adjust to his surroundings as he becomes accustomed to this strange new world he has been thrust into.

YOUR CHILD'S
BRAIN

The best parenting is in sync with a baby's developing brain. Lower brain development in infancy relies on warm, sensory, social experiences. Closely nurtured babies develop neurobiological capabilities that increase their chance of long-term health and happiness.

Baby massage
Gentle massage helps your
baby to relax while deepening
the bonding process.

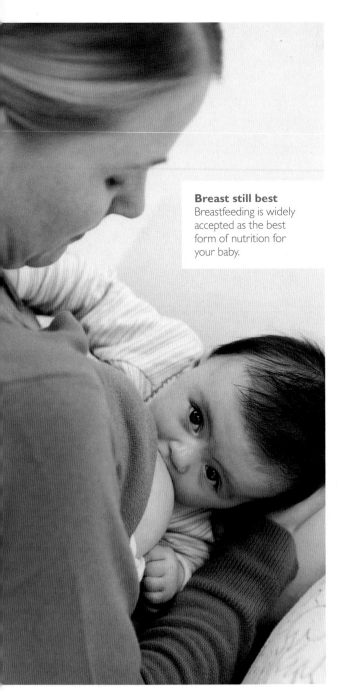

Breast still best
Breastfeeding is widely accepted as the best form of nutrition for your baby.

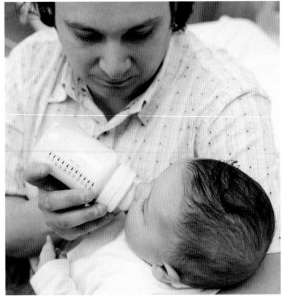

Dad's turn
Giving expressed breast milk from a bottle means dads do not have to be excluded from the feeding routine.

The best food

The promotion and popularity of baby formula in and around the 1960s made breastfeeding seem passé in many parts of the world for several decades. Now, thanks to a better understanding of the benefits of breast milk and campaigning from groups such as La Leche League, breastfeeding is once again acknowledged as being the best source of nutrition for babies and is more widely practised than ever. The World Health Organization states that breastfeeding has been shown to have health benefits that extend into adult life.

I would urge any mother who is able to breastfeed to do so. Breast milk has many benefits: it is easily digestible, provides ideal nutrition, and contains antibodies that help to protect the newborn from infection and disease. Equally importantly, the process of breastfeeding strengthens the bond between mother and child. Dads can also bond with their babies while feeding expressed milk from a bottle. If you are unable to breastfeed, you can still strengthen your bond by holding your baby close, gazing into her eyes, and talking soothingly to her while she bottle-feeds.

Next to his skin

A baby's skin is incredibly sensitive. Nappies and clothing should be made of only the finest natural cotton or other fine natural fibres to avoid skin irritation. Choose clothing that is well-made and avoid fussy garments made from synthetic fabrics.

Always keep your baby's comfort the top priority rather than buying high-fashion clothes that you think will make him look cute.

Another issue relating to skin irritation is the way some babies tend to scratch their faces during their first few months as they learn to explore their bodies with their hands. Keep your baby's fingernails short to allow him to explore, instead of covering them. Later on your baby will like to explore his feet, so keep his toenails short, too.

At first your newborn may enjoy being swaddled in a light wrap while he adjusts to life outside the womb. After a week or two, unwrap your baby and leave his feet and hands uncovered when he is inside the house so he can begin to kick freely and gain control of his hands.

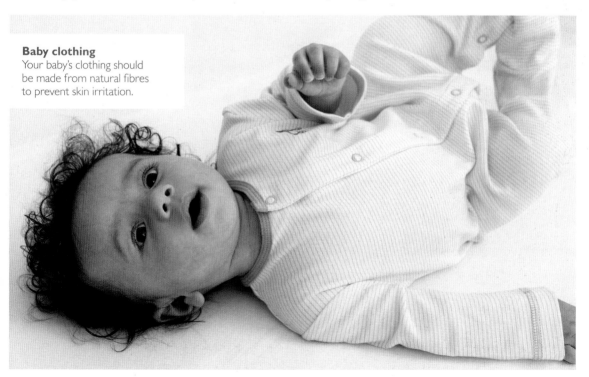

Baby clothing
Your baby's clothing should be made from natural fibres to prevent skin irritation.

Choosing nappies

Parents are strongly encouraged to use soft cotton nappies from birth, rather than the disposable ones that have become so common. Three good reasons for this outweigh the extra work of washing nappies or the expense of using a nappy laundry service: first, the widespread use of disposable nappies has built up mountains of slowly decaying material and untreated waste in every city's sanitary landfill; secondly, natural cotton is less irritating to a baby's skin; and finally, babies in cotton nappies can easily sense that they are wet and so learn to recognize when they urinate. This recognition is important when your child is developmentally ready to begin using the toilet (see pages 92–93).

The need to sleep

Infants sleep a great deal. Like adults, they sleep to give their bodies rest and to allow their minds to process and integrate the sensory impressions and experiences of the day. Sleep is essential to infants for both their physical well-being and their mental health. Babies will often drift off to sleep when they are tired or if they are overwhelmed with sensory impressions. Until recently, your baby lived inside the womb: a warm, comfortable, dimly lit world with only soft sounds and no rough edges. Now her world is filled with bright lights, loud noises, unexpected movement, and strange things that touch her skin. Inevitably, there are times when all of this stimulation becomes too much and she switches off and goes to sleep.

Your baby does not need to be held as she goes to sleep. She may, however, like to know that you are close by. You might like to place a large piece of fleece, a small futon, or a small mattress for your baby in each room where your family regularly congregates. This allows your baby to be where the action is. She will be comforted to be near you, and to hear your voices, and interested to see movement around her. She can look and listen, and then drift off to sleep whenever she is tired.

"Don't wake a sleeping baby" is an old saying, passed down from mother to daughter for generations, and it makes sense. Let your baby sleep. Avoid moving her abruptly or roughly when she's sleeping, keep the lights down low, and speak in soft voices around her.

Ditch the disposables
Soft cotton nappies are gentler on your baby's skin and reduce waste.

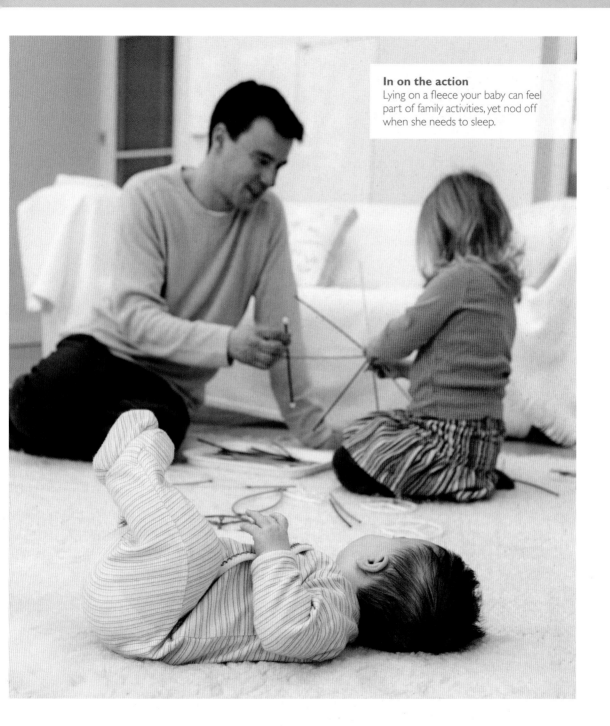

In on the action
Lying on a fleece your baby can feel part of family activities, yet nod off when she needs to sleep.

your
growing baby

In his first year your baby grows and changes rapidly. Take the time to respond to and celebrate each new development.

Montessori had a simple approach to babies. She believed we should:
• respect all babies as individual human beings
• allow them as much freedom of movement and choice in their activities as possible
• and help them to become independent by creating a safe, child-friendly environment that makes it easier for them to explore.

For the first month or so, babies tend to have limited control of their movement. Their arms and legs move jerkily, and they cannot hold their heads upright, which is why we must always be careful to support them. Then, all of a sudden it seems, they discover their hands, feet, and faces and are fascinated by them.

By three months, babies can often raise their heads and chests when they are on their stomachs. They make a grab for objects that are dangling and they grasp and shake hand toys. By seven months they are playing with their toes and reaching for objects. Now everything is going into their mouths or is being banged against the floor. With a little help they can sit up. Babies are usually crawling about on their hands and knees and can pull themselves up to stand by their first birthday. They may be able

A new discovery
Hands soon become a major source of comfort and exploration for young babies, so keep nails short and hands free.

Ready for action
Before long, your baby is rolling over and making his first moves towards becoming mobile.

to take a few steps while they hold onto the furniture, stand alone momentarily, and can walk if you hold their hands and walk with them.

In their second year, babies become increasingly mobile and capable. You will start to notice your child's in-built drive for independence becoming more and more apparent. For example, he will

begin to hold a cup by himself and drink without always making a mess. He will also start to hold out a hand or foot while he is being dressed. It quickly becomes clear, even before your baby begins to move around the house on his own, that redesigning your home environment with your child in mind is going to be an important next step.

making your home
child-friendly

Even in the early days, babies and small children should enjoy
a strong sense of belonging in the family home.

When thinking about how to make our homes more
in keeping with the Montessori approach, we need to
recognize the significance of the things that we bring
into them, especially those our children will experience
in their first three years. Young minds absorb all
impressions like sponges, and in this period before
language develops, their sensory experiences are the
sum total of their world. Keep two objectives in mind.

• Organize your home to help your child become
more independent and self-confident, always
keeping health and safety in mind.

• Design a home that conveys a sense of beauty,
order, and calm throughout.

Take a look at the size of things in your home.
Quite logically, the furniture we use and the way
our homes are arranged are designed for adults –

Free to roam
Babies need to move about and explore in
order to learn. Creating a child-safe environment
will mean your baby is free to do this.

sinks and toilets, tables, chairs, sofas, and beds are all at a height intended for adults. But babies and young children are very small. Without turning your home topsy-turvy, try to modify the rooms where your family gathers to accommodate the needs of your youngest child.

Safety matters

Safety is, and must always be, a primary concern, but children also need to be given the freedom to move around and explore. Your goal is to prepare your home environment to make it safe for babies and toddlers to do just that, under your supervision, but without you having to worry every minute that something terrible is about to happen. Many parents are overly concerned about safety and this leads them to confine their young children in restrictive baby and toddler devices, such as cots, playpens, baby seats, highchairs, swings, pushchairs, and the like. It is not uncommon to see a child strapped into a baby carrier, which snaps into a car seat, which in turn snaps into a pushchair, allowing the child to be carried around without any physical movement and without any human contact.

On one level it sounds reasonable to confine children because of safety concerns, but parents also need to understand that every hour spent confined in a baby carrier is an opportunity lost. Given more freedom, their babies could have been developing muscular coordination and strength, along with the sensory stimulation of hands-on learning. By paying meticulous attention to making your home child-safe, you can create an environment in which your child is free to move about and explore without you having to worry.

"Safety is a primary concern, but children also need to be given the freedom to move around and explore."

SAFETY SENSE

There are many different products on the market that help make your home safer. Here are just a few things to remember.

• Cover all electrical sockets within reach of your growing child.

• Install safety gates to secure your child's bedroom, stairways, and any rooms that you do not want her to enter (or leave).

• Secure or remove any wires that run across the floor or anywhere else where your growing child might reach them.

• Some houseplants are poisonous if eaten. Remove them.

• Remove or lock cabinets or cupboards where you store chemicals, tools, forks, knives, and other potentially dangerous items.

• Use the safety lock or switch on your oven if it has one. Keep saucepan handles to the back of the hob when cooking.

• Bathrooms can be dangerous (especially toilets, hairdryers, razors, and the like). Secure your bathroom from unsupervised exploration, and keep cabinets containing medicines locked at all times.

planning the perfect
first bedroom

Create an organized yet interesting first bedroom that will be fun as well as safe for your baby to explore once he is on the move.

Babies absorb everything that surrounds them in their environment. They are acutely aware of colours, patterns, sounds, textures, and aromas. When planning your baby's first bedroom you will want to provide an environment that is filled with beauty. It should be bright and colourful, clean and orderly. With this in mind, look at the room from your baby's perspective. Get down on the floor.

What do you see? What can you hear? The first few weeks and months will be the time in your baby's life when everything is fresh and new, and lifelong impressions will be made. Bring together elements that are well-made and chosen for their beauty.

Visual stimulation

At birth, babies' eyes tend to focus on objects that are fairly close, but they can also see and are stimulated by something that is further away, especially if it moves. One of the first things babies see and focus on instinctively is the human face. Your presence and interaction with your baby is a powerful source of visual stimulation. As the days go by, his interest in the sights around him grows.

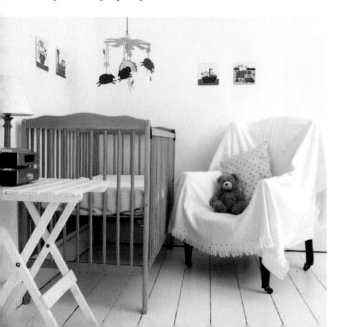

Bedroom basics
A first bedroom should be calm, clean and orderly with bright pictures and mobiles hung at the right height for your baby to enjoy.

Hang a mobile over your baby's bed and his nappy-changing area so he has something to observe. Home-made mobiles with objects that can be changed give your baby fresh things to look at from time to time.

Artwork

Decorate the walls of your child's room with pictures hung very low on the wall (equivalent to eye-level when he is old enough to toddle). Avoid the typical cartoons and commercial images from television and films. Instead, choose framed art prints or posters that show lovely scenes with children and animals. During these years of acute sensitivity, it is worth exposing your child to good art and beautiful objects.

Musical value

Music should be an important part of every child's life, and there is real value in exposing young children to a wide variety of music. Set some space aside, out of your baby's reach, for a sound system to play music for your baby to listen to. Select music that has simple melodies and clearly defined instrumentation when possible, such as recordings of a bamboo flute, a classical guitar, or a harp. Don't overstimulate your baby with loud music – play it at a moderate volume.

Beautiful toys

Babies do not need many toys in the early months, other than a few rattles and a soft toy or two. But as the months pass by, you will probably find your child begins to accumulate more. There is no need to buy expensive battery-operated toys, especially for children under the age of three. Instead, look

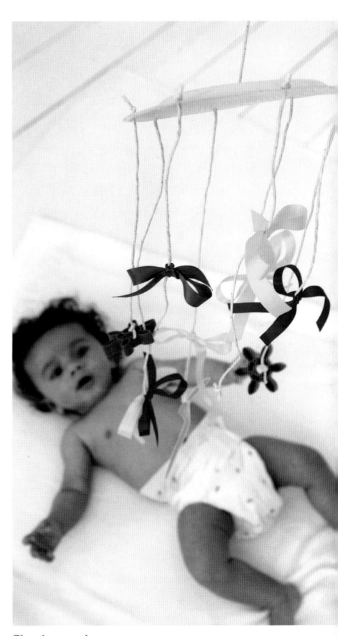

First impressions
Attract your baby's attention and stimulate his vision with a mobile hung out of reach over his bed or nappy-changing area.

37

Easy access
A low bed or futon placed on the floor will give your baby more freedom once she is mobile.

for toys that are well made and which your child can stack, assemble, or interact with in one way or another. Avoid any toy that simply does something while your child watches. You want to encourage your child to be actively engaged, not a passive observer waiting to be entertained.

Choose well-made wooden toys rather than the plastic variety found in every modern toy shop. Remember that your very young child is in a sensitive period during which he is forming strong sensory impressions. Plastic toys are more or less unbreakable and they are relatively inexpensive, but they do not appeal to children in the way that well-constructed, attractive wooden ones can, and they tend to be treated carelessly. One of our goals is to instill a sense of appreciation for beautiful things in our children from the earliest years, while at the same time cultivating a sense of order.

Instead of using a toy box, keep toys neatly on shelves. If a toy consists of lots of small parts, keep them together in a basket.

An infant and toddler bed

For your baby's first bed you will need a cot or, alternatively, consider placing a small futon or mattress on the floor. A low bed of this sort will be just the right height for your child to crawl out of and back into when she is old enough to move around. Freely exploring her bedroom, assuming that you have made it completely safe, is much more interesting than being confined to a cot. Your child's entire bedroom can become a safe play area – all you need is a stairgate across the doorway, safety covers for your electrical outlets and some careful thought about what you bring into the bedroom while your child is young. Use sheets and blankets for your baby's bed, progressing to pillows and duvets only when your child is at least one year old.

A low futon with a waterproof covering is also a safe alternative to the traditional nappy-changing table – it isn't difficult to imagine your baby falling off a changing table once she can wriggle around.

Tidy toys
Keep your child's toys on shelves she can easily reach rather than putting them out of sight in a toy box.

39

adapting your home to a growing child

As your child becomes more independent and busy, try to accommodate her activities wherever the family gathers.

Left to their own devices, young children may tend to create chaos, but they also have a tremendous need and love for an orderly environment. Try to arrange the rooms where your child spends most of her time to make it easy for her to maintain a neat, well-organized atmosphere. It is surprising what an impact this can have on her developing personality.

In the family room

Family room, living room, playroom – whatever you call it, families tend to congregate in one room in the house. Plan yours with your child in mind. It should include accessible shelves where she can keep books and toys neatly and attractively organized. Avoid putting out too many toys and books at one time. Divide toys into three or more sets: favourites, which are kept out on the shelves continually, and two or more sets that are rotated in and out of the toy cupboard every month or so to ring the changes.

Provide a child-sized table and chairs where your child can work on neat projects. Furniture should be at the right height to support good posture while your child reads, writes, and works. Include a basket holding some small rugs that can be spread out to define your child's work areas when she chooses to play with her toys on the floor (see page 85).

In the kitchen

If at all possible, once your child reaches about two years of age, make room in your kitchen for a child-sized work table for young cooks. Use a bottom drawer to store forks, knives, and spoons and a low shelf to hold your child-sized plates, bowls, glasses, and napkins. Set aside the bottom shelf in your fridge for your child. Here you can store small drink jugs, pieces of fruit, and the ingredients she might need for making snacks. Use non-breakable plastic containers to hold peanut butter, jams, lunchmeats, and spreads.

Child-friendly space
Accessible shelving and baskets for storage allow children to maintain an organized environment for themselves.

Kitchen craft
A child-sized work table in your
kitchen allows your child to work
and play alongside you.

Step up
Children need to be able to reach
the sink – make sure your bathroom
step is sturdy and solid.

A child of two is capable of opening the fridge
and taking out her own prepared snack or cold
drink stored in a cup. A slightly older child can
pour her own juice from a jug and make her own
snack (see pages 106–07). Prepared snacks, such
as yogurt and cheese, can be bought in small
individual servings and stored on this shelf.

In the bathroom

Cast your eye around your bathroom to see how
you can make it easier for your child to use what
she needs to. She should be able to reach the basin,
turn on the taps, and reach her toothbrush and
toothpaste without help. There should be a special

place where her towel and facecloth are kept
so she can reach them. Most parents provide
bathroom stools, but small, wobbly stools do not
provide enough secure, comfortable space for
bathroom tasks. If possible, build or buy a sturdy
platform 15–20cm (6–8in) high that fits around
the toilet and basin.

In the hall

Make your hall child-friendly by providing
a low bench where your child can keep her
shoes neatly pegged together with clothes
pegs, and position coat hooks at a level that
she can reach by herself.

In the bedroom

As your child reaches the age of two, you could either continue to allow her to sleep on a futon or buy a bed that is low to the floor. This makes it easy and safe for your child to get into and out of bed on her own, and helps to give her a sense of independence. As long as your child is more than one year old, you may choose to allow her to use a duvet or sleeping bag on her bed instead of sheets and blankets. This makes it much easier for her to straighten and tidy her own bed in the morning.

In addition to providing child-sized furniture, make sure your child can reach door knobs and light switches without help. Light switches can be modified with extenders to allow your child to turn lights on and off independently – these are sold in most hardware shops.

Plan your child's bedroom up to a point, but then let it reflect her personality and current interests. As well as space to play with toys, provide an art table for non-messy art work, such as drawing or paper and paste projects. Hang a notice board low on the wall so your child can pin up her best pieces of artwork. Small shelves and tables also make good display areas.

Music should be an important part of every child's life. Provide a collection of favourite music and songs on a player in the bedroom and give your child a step-by-step demonstration of how to use it carefully and sensibly.

Hall order
Easy-to-reach coat hooks, a low bench, and a stool help your child to get ready by herself.

An orderly environment
When everything has its set place your child can easily maintain order in her room.

A piece of heavy plywood on a low table makes a good base for a child to create a model town or farm with buildings, figures, and animals.

Avoid clutter. Place toys with many pieces in appropriate containers, such as plastic boxes with lids or small baskets. Have a look at the shelves in our Montessori classroom (see pages 20–23) and try to duplicate the look. Store building blocks in a colourful and sturdy canvas bag with handles. Sew on strips of Velcro to fasten the bag closed. When you travel it is easy to pick up the bag full of pieces and take it with you.

IN PRACTICE Bedroom design

A room where everything is accessible and well maintained will help to foster your child's independence, care and respect for possessions, and responsibility for her own space.

Open storage
Small baskets are ideal for toys with lots of pieces and enable your child to tidy up herself.

Pencil box
Keep pencils sharpened and stored in a box that is easy for your child to reach and carry around.

Nature's display
Provide space for a nature museum where your child can collect natural objects she finds.

Basketware
Instead of a chest of drawers, install a low shelf unit on which you can place small baskets for socks and underwear.

Low shelving
Store toys on low shelves, then set up a rotation system so that not all her toys are available for playing with at the same time.

Coat rack
Mount a coat rack low on one wall so your child can hang up her coat, hat, and dressing gown, and get them down easily by herself.

STEP-BY-STEP Painting a picture

Painting does not have to be a messy activity. Set up an art corner where spills can be mopped up, have equipment organized, and demonstrate a set of steps to follow each time your child paints.

One
Fred puts on his plastic overall, spreads out newspaper and pours his paint into wide-necked pots.

Two
It took some practice at first, but Fred is now able to attach a sheet of paper to his easel with a clip.

Three
Fred lets the drips fall from his brush and scrapes the excess paint on the edge of the pot before he starts.

Four
When he has finished he uses clothes pegs to hang his picture on a drying rack, puts lids on the paint containers, and washes out his brushes.

An arts and crafts area

Most of us are keen to encourage our children's creativity. Every home with young children benefits from some sort of arts and crafts area. This might be in a corner of the kitchen, your child's bedroom, or a hallway – really it can be any place where you are comfortable allowing your child to work with art materials, such as paints and pastels, which obviously can spill and stain. You will probably want to choose an area with a tiled floor so that spills can be easily cleaned up, or you can lay down a large plastic sheet or mat.

It is a good idea to set up an easel for painting and an art table covered with a washable tablecloth for drawing, craftwork, and working with clay. A small shelf unit at a height your child can reach can be used to store his art supplies, brushes, paper, and so on. You might want to add in a freestanding clothes-drying rack so your child can hang up his finished paintings to dry with clothes pegs. Once the arts and crafts area is set up, show your child how to proceed using the same step-by-step process each time for getting started and for clearing up when he has finished.

It is important to provide the very best art materials – paints, brushes, drawing pencils, crayons, paper, and such like – that you can afford, and to teach your child how to use them correctly and how to take care of them, including how to store them properly when they are not being used. Depending on your child's age, the art supplies that you prepare might include washable magic markers, crayons, paste, paper, fabric scraps, and recycled household articles for making collages. Children's art supplies can be neatly stored in separate plastic containers.

You can keep tempera paint fresh once it is mixed by storing it in plastic containers with lids, and keep modelling clay in individual sealable pots to preserve the different colours and prevent it drying out. Invest in an easy-to-use pencil sharpener and show your child how to use it to keep pencils ready for use.

ART APPRECIATION

Encourage your child to display his finished work for the rest of the family to see. While the fridge is a time-honoured art gallery, you can give special prominence to his favourite paintings. Buy some easy mounts and frames, and help your child to mount and hang his artwork in other places around your home. Properly mounted and framed, a child's art takes on an entirely different appearance and invites respect. Be prepared to update them regularly with his new work.

watch and follow your child

As parents we often feel the need to direct our children, but Montessori believed we should follow them instead.

Making notes
Keeping a journal of your child's favourite activities will help you track how his skills develop and how his interests change.

How much time do you spend watching your child? I don't mean watching half-heartedly while you are doing something else. I mean focusing your attention completely on your child for an extended period of time. There is no better way to begin using Montessori's principles in your home than by sitting back and observing what your child is looking at, what he says and what he does. Children have so much to teach us about their needs and interests if we will only take the time to pay attention.

How to observe

You may find it useful to keep a bound notebook or journal in which you can make notes and keep a record of your observations. Regularly set aside some time to observe your child. Sit somewhere comfortable close to him so that you can easily see and hear him and any other children with whom he is playing. Make notes every so often about what you see – these will accumulate to form an interesting record of your child's behaviour at different ages, as well as helping you to notice if a pattern of behaviour is emerging at a particular time. Try to interpret what your child's behaviour means. When you notice a new fascination, think about ways to introduce some new activities that will feed and extend this interest.

What to observe

Remember, the only thing that you can count on day after day with children is that as they grow their preferences, interests, and abilities change in unpredictable ways. Every time you observe your child, try to forget about previous experiences or perceptions and stay in the moment, focusing on what is really happening right now.

While your child is playing, notice which toys he selects. How does he use them? Does he tend to play alone or with others? Do you notice any patterns over time? Observe how your child moves about the house. Does he move from place to place quietly and gracefully or with considerable disruption? Is there a room in your home that your child prefers to be in? Can you identify what seems to attract him to that room?

When eating, note what your child most enjoys. Can he drink without spilling and use a fork, knife, and spoon appropriately and with good hand–eye coordination? How does your child behave at mealtimes? Is this a time when he particularly enjoys talking to you about his day?

As you observe, think twice before you interfere with anything your child is doing. Your goal in this exercise is to learn from what he is doing, not to keep jumping up and correcting him.

On a mission
Watch how your child moves around the house and explores. Is she quiet and cautious, or noisy and fast?

2

discovery through the senses

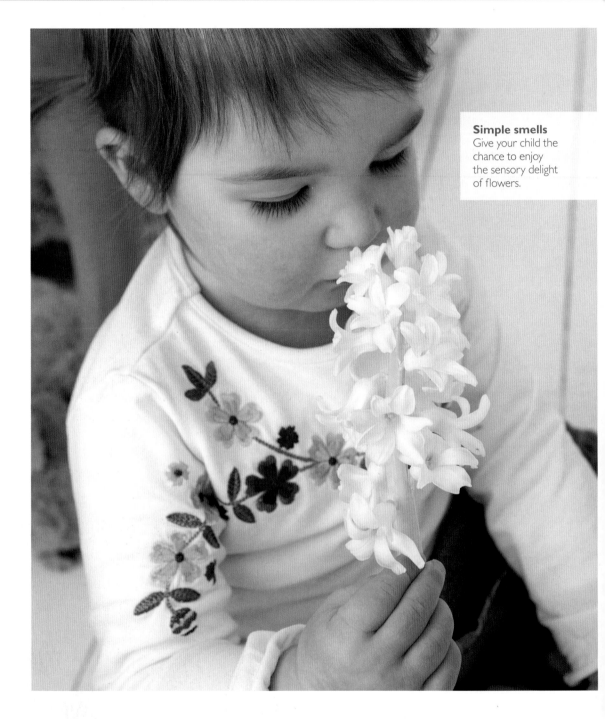

Simple smells
Give your child the chance to enjoy the sensory delight of flowers.

building sensory
awareness

There is an old saying that children learn what they
live. Essentially, Montessori is saying the same thing.

We have already described how babies interact
with the world through their senses from birth.
Montessori believed that we can build on this
by encouraging babies and young children to
focus their attention on the physical world,
exploring with each of their senses – sight,
hearing, taste, touch, and smell – subtle variations
in the properties of given collections of objects.
Exercising children's senses, by creating
opportunities that draw their attention to aspects
of everyday life or through specific sensorial
activities, can greatly improve their awareness.

Boosting brain power
In the years from birth to six, exercises to develop
sensory awareness are especially valuable because
this is when the nervous system is developing.

As we stimulate children's senses in ways that require
them to notice and discriminate between the
properties of different objects, signals are sent from
the nervous system to the brain and back again. The
more this happens, the stronger the neuropathways
in the brain become, as the brain receives important
stimulation that is essential to proper functioning.
Learning how to learn (the assimilation, integration
and application of knowledge) later in life depends
on whether or not the brain was properly "hard-
wired" from an early age.

Tactile discovery
The beauty of simple wooden
puzzles is that they focus all the child's
attention on the shapes of objects.

how babies experience their world

Through the early months, babies increasingly look at, listen to, pick up, taste, and smell almost anything that comes into their environment.

Your child's sensory education began at birth as you held her in your arms for the first time, and cuddled her against you. Her exposure to sensory experiences continued as she took in the comforting aroma of your skin; the sights and sounds and smells of everything around her; the touch of clothing against her tender skin; and the taste of the first solid foods that passed through her lips.

Babies are keen observers in their first few years of life. Everything a baby sees will make an impression, stimulating the brain and nervous system, as well as impacting on the baby's sense of safety and security.

> "Your child's sensory education began at birth as you held her in your arms."

Keen vision

One way we prepare our home environment for babies is by selecting things that will visually stimulate them. It helps, though, to understand something about how vision develops in babies.

When they are born, and for the first month or so, babies' eyes tend to focus on objects about 30.5cm (12in) away. If you watch closely, you will probably notice that your baby's eyes wander and may even cross from time to time. Of all the things they may see, they respond to the sight of the human face most of all, especially the faces of their parents and any other primary care givers. They tend not to notice subtle colours or shading and seem to pay the most attention to things that show clear patterns with high contrast, especially things that are black and white.

At about three months old, babies are beginning to focus on things that are further away. They will watch people's faces intently. Their eyes follow moving objects. Now they can recognize familiar

Sensorial start
Touching, hearing, and smelling
mum signal the start of a child's
sensory education.

Look and learn
Young babies are keen to explore with their eyes and hands in the early months of life.

people and objects at a distance. They begin to reach for things that they see. By about seven months they have developed full colour vision and fairly mature distance vision, and can easily track moving objects with their eyes.

There are all sorts of things that you can do to help develop your child's visual perceptiveness. Talk to your baby, and when you do, make direct eye contact with her and notice how she responds. Look at things together and talk about what you see. Mobiles, as they slowly spin, present an everchanging view of interesting objects that are moving. You might like to have two or three of them around the house and rotate them every so often to create interest and delight in the new sights.

Musical impact

Listening to music is an important sensorial experience. You can introduce your baby to music in many ways. Some parents begin by singing and playing recorded music to their developing baby during pregnancy, sensing that their unborn child can hear sounds and rhythms, just as we can when we are underwater.

In the early years, the experience of hearing recorded music is certainly taken in by babies and young children and is stored as part of the ongoing stimulation from the environment. Talk and sing to your baby from birth. Melodies and lullabies are important and become deep-rooted memories of early childhood. The sound and rhythm of the music that you play in your young child's room and the words to familiar songs that she will begin to learn as she gets older, all lay the foundations for a music education.

Music has also been shown to be directly connected to the development of those areas in the brain that are associated with mathematics and pattern recognition. In other words, exposure to music not only makes children more sensitive artistically, but also makes a real contribution to their brain's development.

Hand to mouth

From her very first feed, your baby's mouth becomes a source of exploration and pleasure. Weaning your baby is about much more than introducing solid food – each new food generates interest and excitement as she explores tastes and textures. As she grows, every object within her reach will go straight into her mouth.

Getting a balance

In no time at all, your baby is able to pick up objects and explore their weight, texture, and temperature. She will use her hands, eyes, ears, mouth, and nose to investigate everything that crosses her path. And

by the time she is one year old, your child will become increasingly curious and able to focus and concentrate, watching or examining something that catches her attention with infinite patience.

It is important to avoid over- or understimulation – babies are good at letting us know how they are feeling. Too much stimulation and they become stressed and tend to go to sleep. They also tend to fall asleep when there is too little stimulation. Ideally, we need to establish a good balance.

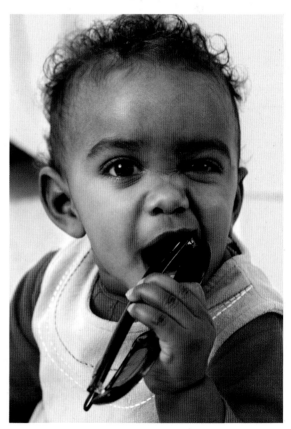

Tastes good
By six months, everything within reach seems to end up in your baby's mouth.

YOUR CHILD'S
BRAIN

Sound is a keenly developed fetal sense – while most noises reaching the womb are muffled, a mother's voice reverberates clearly through her body. Studies show that songs and music played regularly after the 25th week of pregnancy are recognized after birth.

basket of
treasures

All around your baby is a magical world of everyday objects just waiting to be discovered and explored.

Once your baby is able to sit and hold things she will love to explore a "treasure basket". This is a low basket or sturdy box you have filled with lots of interesting household objects and things from nature. The objects must be large enough not to be swallowed and free from sharp edges or anything else that might be harmful when they are touched and quite possibly mouthed by a young child. Older toddlers enjoy the basket too – just keep introducing new objects, hiding some in small boxes to intrigue them.

What's inside?

A treasure basket should create a sense of wonder, surprise and discovery. Gather between 50 and 100 objects, each of which has distinctly different characteristics: shape, colour, texture, weight and smell – use your imagination and common sense. You might include things such as a wallet, a large walnut shell, a pine cone, a brush, a feather, a silver bell, a smooth stone.

Babies and toddlers use all of their senses, whereas adults tend to rely on sight. Objects that have a distinct visual pattern or texture on their surface, a distinct aroma, that are cool to the touch (such as a stone) or which make a noise when moved are especially intriguing. To a young child, everything is a new and exciting discovery.

The treasure basket can entertain young children for long periods of time: half an hour would not be unusual. With babies, keep in mind that it is very stimulating, so is best offered when your child is rested and alert. When young children are first exploring the basket it is best not to say a word – just select an object, carefully examine it and put it back in the basket. Your child may reach for it as soon as you put it down or she may choose something altogether different. Stay close to her but allow her to explore things on her own. Children like us to be nearby, but they do not always want us to interfere.

Treasure trove
The treasures in the basket fascinate young children. They will return to explore them over and over again.

IN PRACTICE Hands-on investigation

Babies love to explore real things that are very different from their plastic or soft toys. The treasure basket offers an enticing selection of subtle colours, textures, sounds, and scents.

Tasting
Sucking has been a source of great satisfaction for your baby since birth so expect every object in the basket to be sampled in her mouth. As long as objects are clean, smooth, and safe, you do not need to limit this experience – your baby will decide what tastes good and what does not.

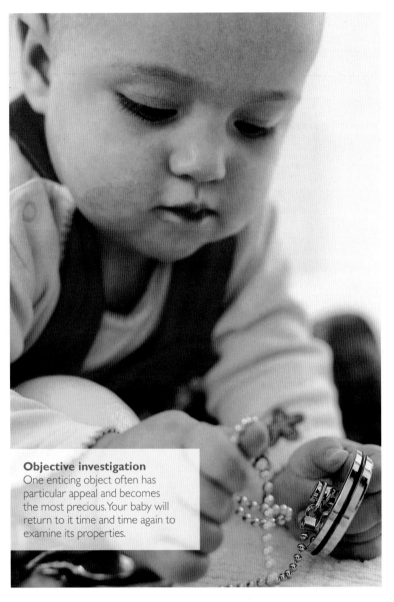

Objective investigation
One enticing object often has particular appeal and becomes the most precious. Your baby will return to it time and time again to examine its properties.

Touching
Things that have a distinct visual pattern or texture on their surface, such as a pine cone, are especially intriguing. Solid glass objects and polished pebbles are interestingly cool to touch, unlike plastic toys, which all feel the same.

Looking
Sharp contrasts were important in the early days when her vision was still developing, but your baby now has adult acuity. She can appreciate natural colours, subtle shades, and combinations of shapes. A simple household item such as a pastry brush can have great appeal.

Hearing
Beans and seeds in small sealed bottles and jars make interesting sounds, as do tiny bells or crackly paper inside tightly tied drawstring bags. Metal chains, strings of beads, and measuring spoons clatter against other objects and jangle when they are shaken.

Exploring
When your child has exhausted the possibilities of the treasure, there is still a textured basket to be investigated. An engaged baby may spend 20 or 30 minutes exploring the contents of the treasure basket – allow her to decide when she has had enough.

Smelling
Your baby has a highly developed sense of smell and will appreciate some carefully chosen scents in the basket. Try bags of herbs, sachets of lavender, and a lemon. Or put scented sweets, vanilla pods, or coffee beans inside a salt cellar.

IDEAS FOR TREASURE

Buy new household items for your treasure basket and wash them before use.

metal: plug and chain • bell • measuring spoon • small whisk

natural: pine cone • sponge • avocado stone • feather • large pebble • shell

wooden: spoon • wooden egg • pastry brush • clothes peg • brick • shoe brush

glass: egg cup • spice jar • salt cellar • small paperweight • string of beads

fabric and leather: satin and velvet ribbons • ball of wool • small purse • silk scarf • pompom • keyholder

rubber and plastic: rubber ball • soap saver • toothbrush • shower puff • bangles

OBJECTS TO AVOID

• small choking hazards

• objects with sharp edges

• objects with loose threads, flakes, or pieces

• anything that might be harmful if mouthed

• materials finished with non-colourfast dyes

sensory activities that help children learn

Exercises that develop children's sensory awareness help them to appreciate their world much more fully for the rest of their lives.

It is important to continue to educate young senses. I don't believe that we can physically improve them through sensory awareness training, but I do think we can help children learn to see, hear, touch, taste, or smell what they experience with a deeper appreciation. In the Montessori classroom an entire area of the curriculum is devoted to sensory awareness training.

At the most simple level, the exercises challenge children to find identical pairs of objects that vary by only one aspect, such as height, length, or width. Other exercises ask them to find identical pairs based on weight, aroma, taste, temperature, or sound. At a more advanced level, children are asked to arrange a set of objects in order based on the variation in one aspect, such as length, height, colour tone, shape, and so on. They find these puzzles and games interesting because they are just difficult enough to represent a meaningful challenge. They are also vocabulary lessons, as the children master the names of everything from geometric shapes to plants and animals. As children learn their correct names, the objects take on new meaning.

The activities in this chapter are simpler but are based on the same principles. Many of the items can be made at home or bought from Montessori equipment suppliers.

"The sensory exercises are just difficult enough to represent a meaningful challenge."

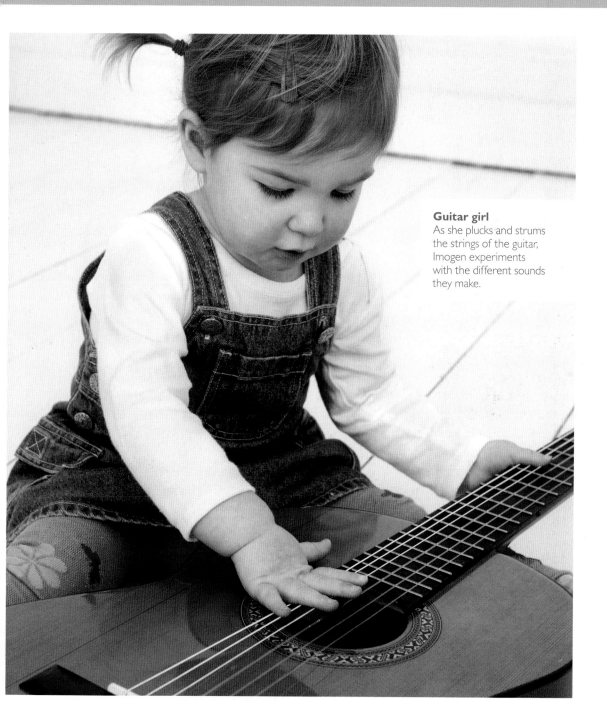

Guitar girl
As she plucks and strums
the strings of the guitar,
Imogen experiments
with the different sounds
they make.

Colour coded
Sorting handfuls of buttons is a pleasing
sensorial activity, stimulating the senses
of sight and touch.

Button mix
You can vary the challenge by introducing buttons
of different sizes and shapes, or made of different
materials, such as bone, wood, and metal.

Colour, shape, and size

Many play activities that primarily stimulate
your child's sight will require him to use other
senses simultaneously.

Sorting objects (2–5 years)

Sorting objects according to shape, size, colour, or
other physical properties is a rewarding activity
that challenges young children to pay close
attention to the task and to make some logical
choices. For this activity, you will want to gather
several examples of some sort of appealing object
in various shapes, colours, and sizes. For younger
children, think carefully about the size of the
objects you choose, to avoid them being swallowed,
or pushed into nostrils or ears. Sets of bricks in
different shapes and colours work well for toddlers.

A good example of this activity for a three- or
four-year-old is button sorting. Buy some buttons
from a haberdashery shop or select several different
sets of four or more identical buttons from your
sewing box, if you have one. Mix the buttons
together in a large bowl then show your child how
to select one button, place it in a smaller bowl and
then find all of the other buttons that match.

Stacking blocks (18 months–3 years)

A good visual sensorial activity involves a set of
wooden stacking blocks that are graduated in size.
Look for blocks or cups that nest inside each other
and stack into a tower that is satisfying to build and
also fun to store away neatly afterwards. Children
learn concepts such as smaller and larger while they
play. In Montessori schools, children around age
three are shown how to use a set of ten precisely
graded blocks to build a pink tower.

STEP-BY-STEP Pink block tower

The bricks are all one colour, so the child focuses entirely on their size. The ten cubes are graduated in size by exactly one cubic centimetre, making it easy to spot which one comes next.

One
Working on a small rug, Lauren looks for the largest stacking cube and uses both hands to place it in position.

Two
The tower has a built-in control of error. If it does not look right and wobbles, it needs a rethink.

Three
Lauren picks up the smaller bricks with one hand. This gives her a muscular impression of their size.

Four
The smooth, painted surfaces make the blocks easy to stack. Lauren sees her tower beginning to grow.

Five
Building is more challenging now. Lauren is careful not to knock the tower as she places the final blocks.

Six
Finally, Lauren places the smallest one-cubic-centimetre cube carefully on the top. Her pink tower is complete.

Wooden puzzle
Choose puzzles with simple cut-out shapes
and with a knob for each piece and offer the
pieces one at a time at first.

Geometric shape stacker (2–4 years)

There are many variations of this toy but most have
one or more spindles and sets of pieces. Once the
pieces are removed, the challenge is for your child
to find the pieces that are alike: squares, octagons
and circles, for example. Then she finds the largest
piece within that set, and places it on the spindle at
the bottom. She continues until all of the pieces have
been placed. Your child should be able to recognize

for herself if she has made a mistake because a
larger piece placed over a smaller one will hang
over, and will not look right.

Simple puzzles (2–5 years)

Simple puzzles are a time-honoured toy for young
children. Always look for puzzles made from wood
with attractive images. Avoid puzzles made of
cardboard and those that do not fit into a frame
for each piece. For children under the age of three,
use puzzles with a large knob for each piece. Resist
the temptation to fit the pieces yourself.

Matching coloured paint charts (3–5 years)

Montessori schools use prepared sets of wooden
tablets painted with various colours to help children
learn to distinguish between primary and secondary
colours and tones, while also mastering the words
used to describe each colour and shade. You can do
this at home by gathering paint charts, which are
usually readily available in DIY stores.

You can create three separate sets of colours
from the charts. Each set should be the same size,
differing only in colour. For younger children start
with a set of six colours, two each of yellow, red,
and blue. Ask your child to match the pairs and
learn the spoken names of these primary colours.

When your child can manage these, collect a
second set of 11 pairs of the primary and secondary
colours and tones: yellow, red, blue, green, orange,
purple, pink, brown, grey, white, and black. Invite
your child to match and name them. For a more
difficult challenge, build a third set containing seven
different shades of each of nine different colours
(yellow, red, blue, green, orange, purple, pink, brown,
and grey), which your child learns to sort in order

from the lightest to the darkest shade. When all of the charts are laid out in an array it creates a lovely display of colour.

There are many ways in which you can make this work more challenging. For example, ask your child to find the colour on the chart that is closest in colour to something in the room. Another challenge is to show your child a colour from the third set of colours and ask him, by memory alone, to point out the colour on the chart that is just one shade lighter or darker. A third activity, with older children, would be to teach them how to create lighter or darker shades of paint by adding white or black paint to an existing colour. By beginning with the pure colour and adding a bit more white and mixing it up, they can create a series of daubs of paint from darkest to lightest, similar to the paint charts. Repeat using black.

Concentration game (3–5 years)

This game helps children develop their visual memory and pattern recognition skills. You can buy various versions at most toy shops or you can make your own. To make a set, cut out 16 pieces of thin cardboard the size of standard playing cards. Either draw or cut out two identical copies of eight different geometric shapes. Pictures of animals can also be used. Glue a shape or picture onto each card. You should now have 16 identical-sized cards, made up of eight pairs of different shapes or pictures.

To play the game, mix up the cards and place them face down in a square made up of four rows down with four cards across in each row. The first player turns over two cards, one at a time. If they match, that player keeps the pair. If they do not match, the player turns them face down again. Players attempt to remember which card is in each position, making it more likely that they will find matching cards when it is their next turn. The game continues until all cards have been matched.

As your child gets better at this game, you can make new sets with different designs or images, and you can increase the challenge by adding more pairs to the set and by not arranging them in rows.

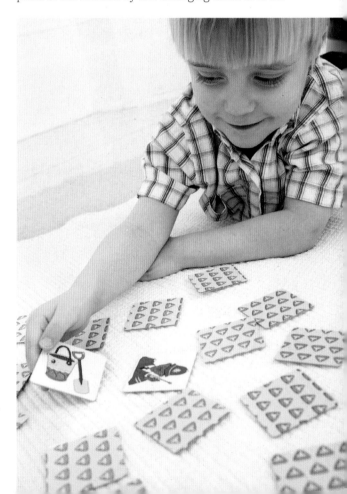

Matching pairs
Remembering where to look to
find each pair of identical cards
tests memory and concentration.

Bean cascade
Butter beans make a pleasant sound when dropped from a ladle into a bowl.

Sound

As your child gets older and his hearing develops, he can learn to distinguish between different sounds and also to pinpoint where a sound is coming from.

Dried butter beans (18 months–4 years)

Find a large salad bowl that is made of heavy pottery or glass and half fill it with dried beans. Dried butter beans are good as they are too large to go into your child's nose or ears, and they make a pleasant sound when dropped into the bowl. Give your child a small ladle and show him how to use it to scoop up some beans, then empty the ladle back into the bowl. Allow very young children to play with the beans. As they swish their hands around, the beans feel nice and make an interesting sound. If your child knocks some out, show him how to pick them up and return them to the bowl. Stress the importance of getting all the beans back into the bowl. At first, don't be surprised if the beans spill all over the place. Show your child the correct way to put them back using patient, kind language.

Matching bells (3–5 years)

For this activity you will need to gather eight or more pairs of bells, each pair having the same sound. Because the bells may look different, your child will need to do this activity with her eyes closed or blindfolded. You are likely to find two types of bells: those with handles and those that are normally sewn or fixed onto something, such as clothing or a horse's harness. The second type is difficult for small children to work with because the ring of the bell is muffled by their hands as they hold it. You can solve this by tying a ribbon to the bell. Your child picks it up by the ribbon with one hand and shakes it or strikes it with the other hand to get it to ring.

Your child rings one bell and sets it aside. She then picks up another bell and rings it to see if it is the same. She may want to ring the first bell again to refresh her memory. If the first bell she tried is not the right match, she sets it aside, selects another and listens to that one for a match. When she finds the right bell, she can set the two matching bells to one side together. She then goes on to select another bell, and repeats the process until she finds the match for each bell.

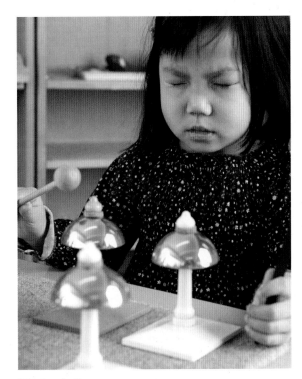

Ringing bells
With her eyes closed, all her attention is focused on the sound of the bells, helping her to match the pairs.

Sound cylinders (3–6 years)

Another exercise that helps children develop the ability to discriminate between sounds involves using a set of sound cylinders. You can make these from any wooden, plastic, or glass containers that you find around the house. The containers need to be opaque so you cannot see what's inside, and they need to produce a clear sound when they are filled with different objects and shaken. Small glass jars, such as the ones that baby food comes in, can be used if you paint the insides of them or line them with coloured paper to make the walls opaque.

Six containers should be painted one colour, and the other six a second colour. Fill pairs of the jars (one jar of each colour) with something that will make an interesting sound when rattled or shaken (dried peas, beans, rice, sand). The children then try to match each green cylinder with the pink cylinder of the same sound. In Montessori schools, each set of six jars of one colour is housed in a box with a lid painted in the same colour.

> "Gradually children develop the ability to relax, listen and appreciate silence."

The silence game (2–6 years)

In our modern world, it seems that silence is almost unknown. It is a great gift to help your child discover the beauty that can be found in silence. When silent we can hear our own thoughts, and we also become much more aware of the world around us.

The silence game helps children develop a much higher level of self-discipline, along with a greater awareness of the sounds around them that most people take for granted. In this activity, get your children's attention either by ringing a small bell or by giving a familiar hand signal to begin a game of "silence". Your children should stop what they are doing, sit down, close their eyes, and try to remain perfectly still. Challenge them to stay like this until they hear you whisper their name. When each child hears his or her name spoken softly, he or she should silently rise and join you. You might want to vary the silence game and help your children learn to move carefully and quickly by challenging them to carry bells across the room without allowing them to ring.

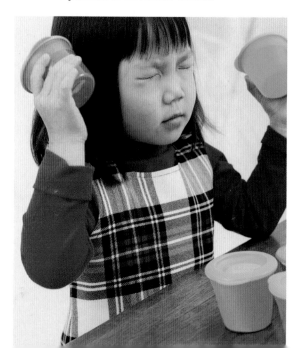

Matching sounds
See if your child can match the sounds made by various objects in pairs of containers.

At first, younger children may not be able to remain still and silent for more than 30 seconds, but gradually they will develop the ability to relax, listen, and appreciate the silence. If your children enjoy this game, make it a daily ritual. Another variation is guided visualization, a process by which your children close their eyes and you describe a scene in front of them for them to imagine: "Now we are walking down to the brook. We put in our toe. Oh my, the water is so cold!"

Listening to music (18 months–6 years)

As your child gets older, you can play all sorts of musical games with her. You can sing or hum loudly along with the music, encouraging your child to do so, too. You can clap your hands to the beat and you can dance freestyle in response to music, swaying, twirling gently, or dancing in any way that feels right for the music playing.

Start to teach your child to recognize the instruments that are being played in a particular piece of music, as well as teaching her the name of the tune – "Mummy, Swan Lake is playing on the radio!" – or even the composer. Make sure your child has access to lots of instruments that she can play – maracas, xylophone, drums, guitar – and encourage her to sing along with favourite tunes.

During these years your child is in a sensitive period for music and has a spontaneous interest in the development of pitch, rhythm, and melody. Musically talented parents who expose their children to live music tend to produce children who are musically gifted. Early signs of precocious talent include remembering melodies, humming or singing in tune, rhythmic ways of moving and speaking, and tapping rhythmically.

Music matters
Offer your child all types of music and share her enjoyment by encouraging her to clap, dance, and sing along.

YOUR CHILD'S
BRAIN

Studies show the value of offering very young children a variety of music in a broad range of tones and pitches. Children begin to distinguish differences in music much as they become able to distinguish their native language from a foreign language.

Touch

There are many ways to train children's sense of touch. We began with the basket of treasures (see pages 58–61) when our children were very young. Preschool children will be ready to attempt some more challenging activities as they start to refine this sense further.

Texture matching (3–5 years)

This game is ideal for helping to develop your child's sense of touch. Typically, it consists of a set of small tablets or squares of wood with a distinct texture on one face, created by gluing a piece of fabric, Velcro, seeds, sand, or other substance to that surface. You will need two matching squares for each texture, creating pairs that feel the same when touched. When the textured side is turned downwards, the squares all look the same. With his eyes closed or blindfolded, ask him to try to "see" with his fingertips, finding the matching pairs. When turned over, the textured sides of each pair match, which provides a visual key so your child can see if he has guessed correctly.

Fabric matching (3–5 years)

A variation on the concept above involves a basket filled with squares of different kinds of fabrics: silk, wool, cotton, tweed, and such like. Prepare matching pairs of each type of fabric. With his eyes closed or blindfolded, ask your child to try to find the pairs of fabric squares that feel the same and to lay them together on the table. When he opens his eyes, he can check his work by looking at the squares.

Sandpaper tablets (3–5 years)

The sandpaper tablets consist of a set of six pairs of wooden tablets with each pair covered with a different grade of sandpaper. Your child attempts to identify pairs that have the same roughness, working by touch alone with his eyes closed or blindfolded. When he has finished matching the tablets, he can check his work by turning them over. The matching pairs will look the same.

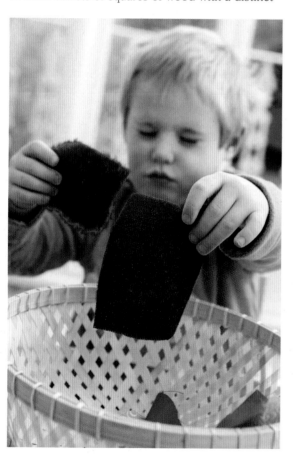

Mix and match
Fill a basket with pairs of different fabrics and see if your child can find the matching pairs with his eyes closed, using his sense of touch.

The mystery bag (3–6 years)

The mystery bag has long been a favourite children's activity. Usually it is simply a cloth bag or box with a hole for your child's hands, through which she can touch and manipulate objects that she cannot see. To play, you will need a collection of small familiar objects that your child can name. While she closes her eyes, place an object inside the bag and challenge her to identify it by touch alone. If your child guesses correctly, switch roles and allow her to choose the mystery object. Make the game more challenging for older children by using different coins, shells, or geometric shapes.

Smell

Children have a much more sensitive sense of smell than most adults. Here are two exercises to help your child refine her perceptions and learn to recognize and name different aromas.

Scent bottles (3–5 years)

These consist of a set of 12 small, identical plastic or glass containers with lids. Cylindrical spice jars with screw-on caps are ideal; you can also use baby food jars. You are going to create two identical sets of six jars. Cover one set of jars with blue paper and the other set with green.

STEP-BY-STEP The mystery bag

This game relies on touch alone, but it is a great vocabulary builder too. Children can describe the shapes and textures they are feeling using words such as hard, smooth, round, and nobbly.

One
Choose objects to go inside the mystery bag that have distinctive sizes, shapes, and textures that you know your child will recognize.

Two
Georgia looks away as she puts her hand into the bag to feel the mystery object. She takes a few moments to explore it with her fingers.

Three
"It is long and thin and has bristles at one end – a pastry brush." Georgia calls out what she thinks it is before pulling it out of the bag.

Put a cotton wool ball inside each jar and place a drop or two of the same scent on the ball of one green and one blue jar. Use different scents for each of the six pairs of jars. You might use aromatic liquid flavourings, such as vanilla, almond, peppermint, and lemon, eau de cologne, or a perfume. In some, you could skip the cotton wool ball and use something solid that has a strong and pleasant scent, such as potpourri, spices such as cloves or cinnamon, chocolate, a strawberry, or orange or lemon rinds. In this case, you need to be sure that your child cannot see what is in the jar. Remember, these substances will dry out and lose their aroma after a while, so you will need to

"Children have a much more sensitive sense of smell than most adults."

refresh them from time to time. Your child selects a jar from one set, opens the lid, and sniffs the scent. She then finds the matching jar from the other set. She puts the two jars to one side and repeats the process with the remaining jars.

Herb scents (3–5 years)

If you have a herb garden, or just a few small pots of herbs on the kitchen window, you can offer some rich sensory experiences with aromatic herbs such as rosemary, lavender, basil, and thyme. It will be even more satisfying if your child has grown some of the plants herself (see page 151). Children enjoy using a small mortar and pestle to crush herbs for cooking. You can also dry herbs together and experiment with scents to make bowls of potpourri or small sachets to put in drawers.

Taste

There are four basic tastes that we can sense with our tongue: sweet, sour, salty, and bitter. The most basic way to introduce the concept of taste

Scent bottles
Comparing and matching scents in bottles that give no clue to their contents helps to refine a child's sense of smell.

is to talk about different foods: "Mmmm, this apple is so sweet!" or "I think this popcorn is very salty! What do you think?" Some children are extremely fussy about eating foods that have a strong or unfamiliar flavour. You may find that your child becomes more willing to try new foods as he explores new scents and tastes through sensory experiences. To start with, gradually introduce each taste with different foods. For example, you might introduce bitter by offering your child a tiny bit of rocket or some parsley. "Some foods taste bitter. Would you like to try my…?"

Another activity would be to suggest that your child pays close attention to the taste of certain foods: "Goodness, just taste and smell the ginger in this gingerbread cookie!" You can suggest that your child closes his eyes, takes a taste of something, and tries to name what the taste is. "This is very lemony, Mummy!" You can also make tasting bottles (see panel below).

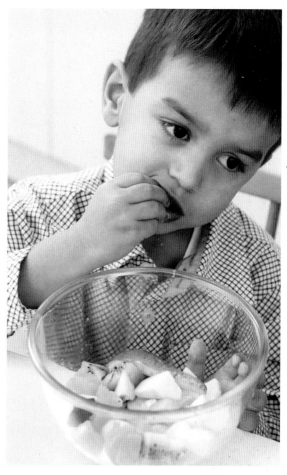

Fruit flavours
Eating fresh fruit salad is a multi-sensory experience for your child, full of colour, scents, tastes, and even sounds as he takes each bite.

TASTING BOTTLES (3–5 YEARS)

Gather six small bottles with squeeze droppers and paint the lids of three bottles blue and the other three red. Now you have two sets of three dropper bottles. Fill one bottle from each set with a liquid that represents one of the basic tastes. For example, sugar water (sweet), lemon juice (sour), and salty water (salty).

Your child should wash her hands, line up each set of bottles, then carefully unscrew the top from one bottle and put a small drop on the back of her left hand. Ask

her to lick it slowly to get the taste. Now she chooses a bottle from the second set, unscrews the lid, and puts a small drop on the tip of one finger on her right hand. Does it taste the same? No? Set this bottle aside and repeat the process until she finds the match then remove both matching bottles and set them aside.

Your child needs to wash her hands before returning to the remaining bottles and repeating the process. When all three pairs have been matched, she's finished.

3

let me
do it

help me to
do it myself

Independence is the greatest drive of a young child. While working to achieve it, children have fun practising and mastering many skills.

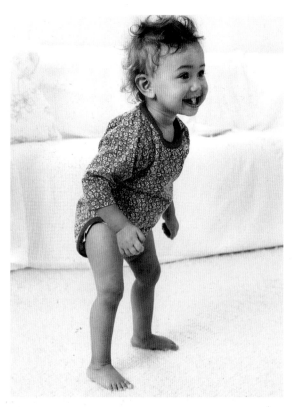

From very early in life, children want to practise the skills that will make them independent. Helping children learn to do things for themselves, from dressing and washing to pouring drinks and making snacks, sets them on the road to independence.

According to their age, young children can be very helpful around the house. They can clean up their rooms, help to chop vegetables, sweep up messes, dust, and generally help us in the kitchen as we cook and bake. They can learn how to set the table, carry food to the table, and arrange flowers and table decorations. They can also learn table manners, how to greet guests at the door, and how to act as nice hosts and hostesses to young friends, guests, and relatives who come to visit. With gentle guidance, children quickly learn to

Stepping out
Mobility brings a first taste of freedom, enabling children to reach higher, move faster, and explore unaided.

work neatly, tidy up after themselves and help out with household chores, and they will thoroughly enjoy practising these skills.

Sense of self

Children who feel respected and competent develop a far greater sense of emotional well-being than children who are doted upon. The activities in this chapter are designed to help you teach your child specific everyday living skills that will help him become increasingly independent and self-confident. Lessons in these skills are intended not only to teach the skill itself, but also to help your child to develop a sense of calmness, concentration, cooperation, self-discipline and self-reliance. Many have social objectives too, teaching self-awareness, sensitivity to others and service to the community. Parents have to set the tone and serve as daily role models for everyday living skills. We need to be poised, purposeful, precise, caring and giving.

According to Maria Montessori, "The essence of independence is to be able to do something for one's self. Such experience is not just play. It is work children must do in order to grow up."

Life lessons

The lessons your child learns can be broken down into three areas:

• care of himself
• everyday tasks around the house
• grace and courtesy (see pages 132–35).

Gaining independence
Watch for the signs that your child is ready to do things for himself and allow him to master new skills.

Many of these lessons involve the mastery of fine motor skills, such as how to fasten a button, pour from a small jug, or carry things without dropping them or stumbling. These are lessons that most parents try to teach their children when they are very young. Hopefully, you will find in this chapter some strategies to help the process go smoothly. Your child can start at any age, whenever you feel he is ready. The best way to know when the time is right for each lesson is to pay attention to what your child is telling you, not only with words but with actions. For example, there comes a point when your child will be eager to hold a cup. That would be the right time to begin teaching him how to drink from it himself.

children love to
work and play

Small children want to be part of your world. For them work is every bit as much fun as play if they are given the chance to do it.

The best way to encourage your child to try new skills is to demonstrate them precisely and slowly in simple ways that he can understand. Then give him time to practise and to be allowed to make his own mistakes and correct them. By giving him clear boundaries and careful guidelines, you can allow him to learn to do things for himself and give him the self-respect and confidence that come with independence.

Try squatting down to take a look at the world from your child's perspective. He is developing his skills in a land of giants where everything is beyond reach or too big to handle.

> "Children need to be shown new skills in simple ways they can understand."

A matter of size
The first step is to seek out tools and utensils that are the right size for your child. Most of the tasks young children can do are much easier if they have equipment made in a size that is right for their age. It is easy to find child-sized toothbrushes, but there are also child-sized cups, plates, forks, spoons, watering cans, brooms and brushes, and even tubes of toothpaste.

The real thing
Why would you buy your child a play kitchen when what she really wants is to be with you helping in the real kitchen? I'm not suggesting that we should turn a three year old loose with a cleaver or oven, but there are many things that are not dangerous that your child can do if you take the time to teach her how. For example, she can easily stir things that are cool, wash vegetables, or learn how to set the table. Children do not always want to do what we are doing,

Real work
Carrying out purposeful tasks in the garden, using the right-sized equipment, is satisfying and fun for a young child.

Setting the table
Buy child-sized cutlery. Outlines of each piece show your child how to set the table and where to place her plate and cup.

and I am not suggesting that you should make a young child wash the dishes when she really wants to play. But when your child asks or shows that she wants to help, be ready to show her how. If you've taken the time to organize your kitchen to provide a small work table and some child-sized basic tools, she is more likely to want to help and to come back again and again.

Step by step

Many of the things that we do every day involve several different skills, each of which we learnt along the way. By breaking tasks down into small steps, you can help your child to master each level

of difficulty one at a time. Take this approach when you want to teach your child how to sort clean socks in the laundry or put flowers in a vase. Think about each step and how you can make it simple to follow. Explain each step with just a few words as you demonstrate it, so your child concentrates on what you are doing rather than what you are saying. Then let your child practise until she is competent at each stage.

Learning to ride a bicycle is a good analogy. When children are ready, parents often give them a tricycle and let them learn how to mount and dismount, how to steer, and how to work the pedals. As safe as tricycles are, they usually do not have brakes, and parents are careful where they let their children ride them. The next step might be a balance bike, which has no pedals. As children push themselves along they lift their feet off the ground and gradually develop balance. Then parents introduce a proper bike, sometimes with stabilizers to help keep this larger bike upright, while children get used to the pedals, steering, and brakes. As children become more confident, they ask for the training wheels to be removed. Before we know it, they are zipping around on their bikes, while we constantly remind them to wear their safety helmets.

Step by step, this process of mastering an everyday skill is made easier by careful planning, patient instructions, and support from parents. Lessons such as these continue as children grow up. The process of teaching your teenager to drive is a good example of an everyday life skill your child learns when she is almost grown. Learning how to deal with conflicts with friends, manage savings, and plan a small party are other examples.

Perhaps one of the most difficult things to do as a parent, once we have taught our children a new skill, is to then allow them to continue to practise this skill as part of their everyday life without interfering. While we would never suggest that a child who has learned to ride a two-wheeler bike goes back to stabilizer wheels, how often do we find ourselves continuing to bundle our children into their coats or shoes long after they are capable of managing to put them on by themselves?

Careful instruction
When we teach a child to ride a bike we choose the right bike at each stage and offer step-by-step instructions.

83

A sense of order

A key element in teaching children everyday life skills is keeping everything tidy. In the crucial sensitive period for order (see page 16), their world needs to be well organized. If taught where things belong and how to return them correctly when they have finished using them, children internalize this sense of order and carry it with them for the rest of their lives.

Most of us can be overwhelmed by the chaos that quickly develops around the house if we leave things lying around. Children are particularly sensitive to this. Although they are often masters at creating a mess, most find it difficult to clean up after themselves. The most efficient approach is to teach them to clean up as they go along. While some children may be born with a "neat gene", they all can be taught right from the start

to work and play in a tidy way without stifling their creativity or stripping playtime of fun. The secret is to establish a ground rule and gently but firmly teach her that while she may select anything from her shelves to work and play with for as long as she wishes, she must return it when she is finished with it, and may not remove something new until the last thing has been put away.

Some toys are better when used together with other toys – a set of building blocks and a collection of toy cars, for example. All you need to do in this instance is incorporate the two toys into a collection. Children can easily learn special rules, such as the idea that the toy cars and blocks go together, and it's fine to play with them at the same time. The key idea is to get all of the toy cars and blocks returned to the shelf before your child goes on to the next project.

Learning order
Teach your child to take one book off a shelf at a time, turn pages carefully without tearing them, and to return the book afterwards.

Photographic labels

Use photos on storage containers to help your child return things to the right place. You can also place a photo on each shelf showing how the entire shelf should look when all the toys, games, books and such like, that are stored there have been placed back in the proper order. This allows your child to use the photo as a control of error (see page 87) whenever she is returning materials to the shelves after she has finished playing or working with them or inspecting them for damage.

Practical storage

As you will recall, I recommend against using toy boxes (see page 39). Set up low shelves to hold your child's books, toys, and games in her bedroom and in those rooms around the house where you and the family tend to spend the most time. Find ways to contain toys with many parts to keep them from going everywhere. Usually this involves using some sort of container that is large enough to hold all the pieces and sturdy enough not to fall apart or look tattered with use. Depending on the nature of a particular toy, a heavy plastic container, a strong basket, a sturdy wooden box, or perhaps a large jar or bowl provide good solutions.

Defined work/play areas

You probably don't want your child finger-painting in the middle of your living-room rug. You certainly don't want her painting on the walls, either. Think about each toy and activity that you are going to make available to your child, and determine where each can be used safely without creating a mess that would be difficult for your child to clean up. Some activities ought to be done in the kitchen or in a room that has a tiled floor that makes it fairly simple to clean up spilled food or paint. Some might be fine to use in the family room, but not where people will have to step over them as they come and go. Still others are outdoor activities, such as woodworking or kicking and throwing balls, and need to be done in the garden.

Establish your plan, then teach your child how to do things correctly rather than punishing or criticizing her for making mistakes. If you find your child using a toy in the wrong place, redirect her to where this activity belongs. If a mess has been made, it is reasonable, depending on your child's age, to expect her to clean it up or at least to help with the tidying up. This often doesn't work well with toddlers. With them, prevention is the only defence. Don't allow them to get access to something that they should not use.

Roll out the mat
Playing on a mat or rug confines activities so pieces don't spread out all over the room.

YOUR CHILD'S
BRAIN

Children thrive on routine and order, but does a messy home affect your child's behaviour? A study of UK families revealed that a chaotic environment was likely to produce bad behaviour in children, over and above parenting. And when parenting skills were poor, a disordered home added significantly to the negative effect on children's conduct.

Some things are fine to work or play with on a sofa; some are best done at a table. However, children often find that for many of the activities they enjoy they are most comfortable on the floor. Give your child small rugs or mats to define her work/play area. Toys and puzzles have a tendency to spread out all over a room if you don't help your child to contain them somehow. A small rug, perhaps 75 x 120cm (2½ x 4ft), defines an excellent work/play area on the floor. For larger projects, such as a giant city built of blocks, your child can use two mats placed alongside each other. Teach your child how to roll and unroll her mat and how to store it in a basket.

Safe manoeuvres

Think about how your child can safely and carefully carry each toy or utensil from the shelf to where she wants to work and play. Often the best way is for her to carry the toy in its own container. Some toys, games or utensils are easily carried by themselves – a doll, for example. Others involve many pieces and sometimes the set is too large or heavy for a child to carry. In this case, provide small trays that your child can use to carry enough pieces to work with in one or more trips. Keep in mind that children do not automatically know how to carry things on a tray without spilling, so you will need to demonstrate and let your child practise. A small basket or a trolley may be easier for a child who finds using a tray difficult.

Pride of ownership

Teach your child to take care of her toys and other belongings. Rather than punishing her if she breaks something, or simply buying a replacement, take the time to show her how to use things correctly. When a toy, game, or anything else is broken, see if it can be repaired, then make that process a lesson itself. Encourage your child to help you repair things and teach her how to do simple repairs herself. Demonstrate how you personally take care of your family home and encourage your children to do likewise on a daily basis. Draw her attention to the small details, such as picking up stray pieces of paper, beads or other debris from the floor.

"When a toy or game is broken, see if it can be repaired, then make that process a lesson itself."

Control of error

Whenever possible, try to build a control of
error into each activity so it becomes clear to
your child when she has made a mistake. The
rationale behind letting children use cups and
bowls that break if they are dropped or misused
is that children quickly learn to be careful and
controlled when they use them. Mistakes are an
opportunity for patiently showing your child once
more how to do a task correctly, and generally
lead to a new lesson in problem solving: "How
do we gather up all those beads?" or "How do
we safely clean up the broken pieces?"

Beauty and harmony

Select toys, tools and other everyday items
that your child will use on the basis of their
appropriate size, ease of handling, and beauty.
When you choose trays, jugs, and other utensils
for your child to use in everyday life skills (see
pages 100–07), avoid things that are cheap and
made of plastic – look instead for the most
attractive materials that you can find and afford,
your child is more likely to take care of them.
Children respond to the beauty of wood, glass,
silver, brass, and similar natural materials.

Young children absorb and remember
every nuance of their early home environment.
The aim is for you to design activities that will
draw your child's interest and to create prepared
surroundings that are harmonious and beautiful.

Beautiful toys
In a world where so much is plastic and
garish, children are drawn to the beauty
of natural materials such as wood.

getting to grips with
bathroom skills

Learning how to take care of herself – from washing hands to brushing teeth – will make your child feel confident and capable.

Many of the skills your child needs to accomplish to look after herself are learned in the bathroom. Look carefully at your bathroom and make any changes needed (see page 43) to ensure this is a safe and comfortable place for your child to try the following activities.

Turning the tap on and off

This is a straightforward task. It requires a small platform in front of the basin your child uses, allowing her to get up high enough to reach across and use the tap. Be sure a small hand towel is close by for her to use to dry her hands.

Show your child how to pull out the plug or open the pop-up drain, and explain that it is very important not to allow the water to overflow from the sink. Show her the cold water tap, and tell her "This is the tap for cold water." Now show her the tap for hot water. Tell her "This tap turns on the hot water. You have to be very careful! The water is so hot that it can hurt you."

Now slowly turn on the cold water, part way, and turn it back off. Invite your child to turn it on. If she turns it on too fast, say "You have to be careful not to turn the water on too fast because it will splash everywhere." Now ask your child to turn off the tap. Don't be surprised if she turns the water on full force when she means to turn it off. The point of the lesson is to teach her how to control the flow of water in a sink. Repeat the

Tap tactics
Learning safe ways to manage running water from a tap is a big step towards bathroom independence.

lesson as needed, emphasizing which one is the cold water tap and which one is the hot, and how to turn the flow on and off gently.

Once your child can turn the cold water on and off, ask her to try the same thing with the hot water. If you have mixer taps, do this with the cold water flowing first. Explain "If we start the cold water first, and then turn on the hot water, they mix and become warm, but not hot." Show your child how to touch the edge of the water flow lightly to see how hot or cold the water is running. Also show her how to adjust the temperature by turning the hot water tap on more completely or reducing its flow. If you have separate hot and cold taps, you will need to show your child how to run some cold water into the sink with the plug in, then turn the hot water tap and add hot water until the water in the sink is warm.

Now both dry your hands, and you're finished. Don't be surprised if your child wants to practise this exercise over and over again for a while.

The wonders of washing
Soap gets germs off your child's skin. Alternatively, show your child how to use use an anti-bacterial handwash in a pump dispenser.

Washing hands
Once your child understands how to work the tap, introduce the idea of using soap and warm water to wash her hands. In the flu and cold season, germs are most often spread when children touch their fingers to their eyes, nose, or mouth. One of the most effective ways to reduce the spread of

Clean face
Make sure your child has her own flannel and towels at a level she can reach. Show her how to squeeze it out before cleaning her face.

FUN WITH WATER

Children love to play in water so it is a good idea to set up a place where your child can play safely. You can use the sink, a bowl or a preschool water table sct up in a room with a tiled floor where spilled water can be easily mopped up. In the summer months, move your water play activities outside into the garden.

Establish and enforce some basic ground rules such as no splashing indoors and not allowing certain objects, such as anything sharp or electrical, in or near the water.

Provide some fun things for your child to play with: waterwheels, boats, a funnel, a small doll to wash, and cups and bottles to empty and fill.

infections is to encourage your child to wash her hands often, scrubbing them with soap under the running water for at least 30 seconds. Soap doesn't kill the germs, but it does loosen the dirt and grime. Hand washing under running water in this way is effective because most, if not all, of the germs on your child's hands are washed off and go down the drain. It never hurts to explain why we do things like this, using simple language and a short explanation.

Brushing teeth

Once your child knows how to use the basin, she needs a small toothbrush and a mirror. Ask your dentist for advice on introducing fluoride toothpaste and on the best way to brush. Now teach your child. The general rule is to brush twice a day; if your family brushes after each meal, wait for 30 minutes before brushing because tooth enamel needs time to reharden after contact with acidic food.

Bath time

Many children enjoy being with mum or dad at bath time and you will want to supervise until you can clearly see that your child is old enough and capable of bathing herself safely. Usually, sometime between the ages of three and five, your child will let you know that she is old enough to bathe herself. Follow her lead, but make sure she knows the correct way to wash her hair and use a face cloth.

Brushing hair

Make sure your child has her own brush or comb and show her how to brush and tidy her hair. If she prefers you to brush it for her, that's fine. As she gets older, she might like to learn how to put in easy-to-use hair clips and bands.

Tooth care
Buy your child a small toothbrush and teach her to brush her teeth correctly, rinse the brush, and put it back in its holder.

Tidy hair
Having her own hairbrush or comb helps her take pride in her appearance. Offer help with tangles, but let her do as much as she can.

90

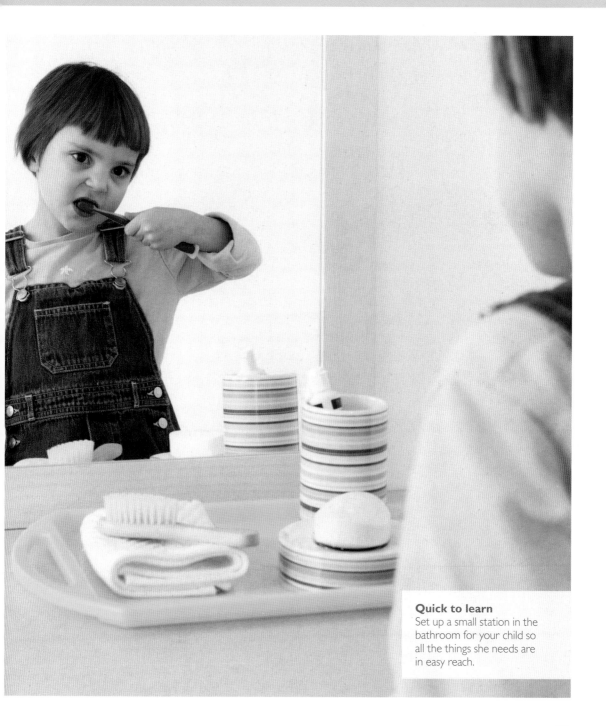

Quick to learn
Set up a small station in the bathroom for your child so all the things she needs are in easy reach.

Introducing toilet training

Learning to use the toilet is a natural process that begins when your child's desire to be grown up and his neurological development have reached the point where he can control his bladder and bowels. We don't train children to use the toilet; we support them when they are ready. Readiness depends largely on the maturation of a child's nervous system, and this tends to vary from one child to another. You cannot hurry the process, and gentle patience is certainly a virtue. But, like so many aspects of living with children, if we understand how things develop, we can prepare the environment and play a supporting role.

It all revolves around your child's amazing brain and nervous system. When children are born, their brains and nervous systems are at an incomplete stage of development. Between birth and 18 months, the cells of the nervous system become coated with myelin, a fatty substance which facilitates the transmission of impulses from cell to cell more efficiently throughout the nervous system. This allows babies and toddlers to gain more and more refined control and coordination of their movements.

This process of myelination, or integration of the nervous system, develops in stages. Babies gain control of their head, then arms and the trunk of their body and eventually legs and feet. From random movements, they gain the ability to move with conscious intent and control.

Toilet curiosity

Children often become interested in toilets when they are about a year old. They like to flush and often want to play with the water in them. If this is the case with your child, give him access to more appropriate water play, such as water in the bathroom sink. About this time, children also become fascinated with their "poo" and "wee". Don't be surprised or offended. Just explain that "Everyone poos – it is how our bodies get rid of the part of what we eat that we cannot use."

By 15 months, many children become interested in dressing and undressing themselves. They often also express interest in wearing pants and may try on their older siblings' or their parents'. This is probably an indication that they are becoming curious about learning to use the toilet.

Around 18 months, children have a much more developed and integrated nervous system and enter a sensitive period in which they can recognize physical sensations and begin to gain control of their bladder and sphincter muscles. At this stage many children have both the physical ability and the interest to control bladder and bowel.

TOILET TRAINING TIPS

• **Be patient** and encouraging.

• **Prepare your bathroom** to support your child's independence.

• **Dress your child in cotton training pants** during the day.

• **Teach your child how to undress**, clean up, flush, and dress again step by step, when he seems ready to start using the toilet.

• **Explain bodily functions** patiently.

• **Keep old towels on hand** so your child can clean up accidents.

• **When accidents occur**, be understanding.

If they are given the opportunity to spend as much time as possible in pants, rather than nappies, they gain a greater awareness of these bodily functions and are much more likely to learn to recognize the sensation when their bladder is full. If you have noticed the signs of awareness in your child, try to dress him in cotton pants, at least when he is at home during the day. He will have the occasional accident, but he will also become acutely aware of it. When children are wearing disposable nappies they can rarely sense when they are wet or soiled.

About now, many children will want to sit on the toilet or potty in imitation of their parents and older siblings, even though they have not yet developed bladder and bowel control. Gently support your child's interest, slowly teaching him how to pull down his pants, sit on the toilet correctly, use toilet paper to wipe his bottom, pull his pants up, flush the toilet, and wash his hands.

Toilet curiosity

Maintaining this toileting approach should be possible at a Montessori childcare facility but I accept that this may not be available to all. For some children training may come later, but the important point is to be consistent when it begins, and ask your child's carers to follow your lead.

Be prepared for occasional accidents even in older children. When they occur, stay calm and be reassuring. Keep clean pants on hand where your child can find them, and provide a hamper, and a stack of old towels for wiping up accidents. Help your child when he requests it or if he is clearly overwhelmed, but don't rush in unnecessarily and make him feel ashamed.

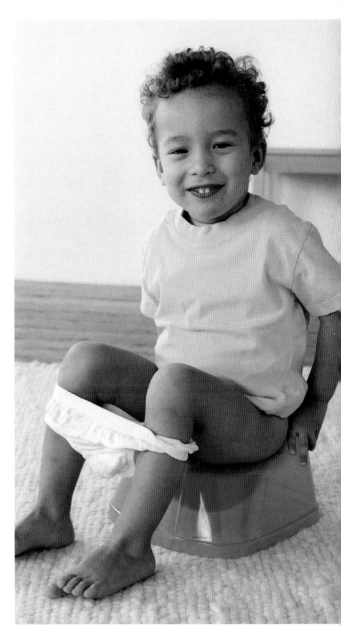

I can do it!
Using the potty is a natural process that grows out of neurological development and the drive for independence.

the art of getting
dressed

In no time at all, your child will be undressing and
dressing herself at a moment's notice.

Somewhere between the ages of six months and a
year, most children begin to hold out a hand or foot
while they are being dressed. At about 18 months,
many toddlers want to start wearing pants like
their older siblings or friends (see pages 92–93).
Some may begin to take delight in dressing and
undressing themselves, and it is not uncommon for
children of this age to try on their older siblings' or
parents' clothing. These are all signs that your
child is ready to start dressing herself.

When your toddler starts to show an interest,
make time for some trying-on sessions with hats,
scarves and slippers. Sit on the floor next to your
child and both put on trousers together, then socks,
and a T-shirt or a jumper. Make your careful
demonstration into a game.

Everything within reach

You will remember when I was describing how to
organize your child's bedroom (see pages 42–45),
I talked about the importance of providing hooks,
hangers, shelves, and baskets that are low enough
so that your child can reach them on her own,
and drawers that she can easily open herself.
Take a close look at her bedroom and make sure
everything is in the right place and accessible.

As children get older and more independent,
it is a good idea to give them choices. Set out
two outfits that your child can choose from each
morning. As the day draws to a close, discuss
with her which clothes she might like to wear the
following morning. You can also help by buying
clothing that is easy for your toddler or young
child to put on and take off by herself. Look for
trousers with elastic waistbands. Avoid clothes that
have lots of buttons or zips until your child is
ready to enjoy the challenge. Choose shoes that
slip on or fasten with Velcro. Try to be patient as
your child learns to dress herself. Young children
need lots of practice, and once they have started
work on their dressing skills, they need to be
given time and opportunity to perfect them.

Complete mastery
Give your child time
to practise, and she
will soon master even
the more complicated
fastenings.

FIRST FASTENINGS

Encourage your child to practise dressing skills before trying them out on her clothes.

Fastening buttons
Allow her to practise buttoning and unbuttoning on a piece of clothing with large buttons, which can be laid out on the floor.

Bow-tying frame
This frame has two different-coloured ribbons, one attached to each side, to help master the skill of tying bows.

IN PRACTICE Getting dressed

The best time to practise getting dressed is when no one is running late or in a rush. Make time for some relaxed trying-on games.

I can dress myself!
At about 18 months your child may start to develop an interest in putting her clothes on by herself.

Getting ready
Putting on simple items such as a hat and a scarf is a good starting point when your child is ready to master the skills he needs to dress himself.

Socks on
Managing to put on his own socks will require manual dexterity from your child. Show him how to get them the right way round and pull them on.

Velcro shoes
Shoes with Velcro fasteners are the easiest for young children to learn with once they are ready to start putting their shoes on by themselves.

Tying laces
Learning to tie shoelaces usually takes practice to perfect. A bow-tying frame (see opposite) is useful when your child starts learning this skill.

97

STEP-BY-STEP · Putting on a coat

This simple method of putting on a coat is effective and fun for children to try. There is something magical about the way the coat slips into place and always ends up the right way round.

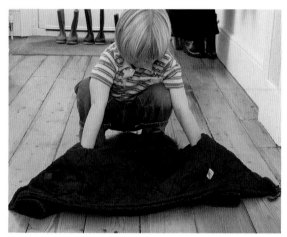

One
Eden lays his coat on the floor with the lining uppermost and squats down at the top where the hood is.

Two
Slotting his hands into the sleeves, he lifts the coat over his head. The sleeves slide down over his arms.

Three
The coat falls neatly down over his back and Eden straightens out the front. "See, I can do it myself!"

Four
Having practised to perfection, Eden can now put on his coat all by himself in less than 30 seconds. He beams with pride.

Putting on a coat can be the most awkward aspect of getting dressed for a young child. From time to time even adults struggle to find a sleeve left hanging somewhere behind. In Montessori nurseries in winter when a large group of small children all need to put on coats at the same time to go outside, there is a simple technique they are taught to help them get ready with the minimum of assistance. This technique is just as easy to use at home (see opposite).

Preparation helps

Start by organizing your hall with shoe racks and a low peg on which your child can hang his coat (see page 42). Show your child how to pull his coat sleeves the right way out each time he hangs it up. Now show him how to put on his coat following the steps in the sequence on the left. Approaching the coat from the collar end is important (many children end up with an upside-down coat the first few times) so demonstrate this step carefully. When your child masters this trick for putting on a coat he will feel a huge sense of independence and achievement, so let him practise as much as he wants to.

"Try to be patient as your child learns to dress himself. Young children need lots of practice."

SHOE ORDER

Getting the right shoe on the right foot is often a problem for young children. Using clothes pegs to clip pairs of shoes together helps to keep shoes and boots neatly in pairs ready for your child to find them easily. When shoes are clipped together properly it also presents her with right and left shoes in the correct position when she is ready to put them on.

helping out around the house

Children naturally want to be with us around the house when they are young. Most want to help, if only to feel useful and more grown up.

If you think of the household chores as a family activity in which children are welcome to participate even when they are very young, you can instill in your children a sense of pride in keeping the house and garden neat and clean. Work should never be thought of as a chore, but as an activity that leads to a sense of order and completion. Obviously, children do not know how to do everything that we can do, and it often seems easier simply to do things ourselves. By taking the time to prepare the environment and to teach children patiently how to do things step by step, you continue the process of teaching skills as well as attitudes about work.

The right approach

Start by gathering equipment; she will need a child-sized broom, mop, bucket, her own feather duster, cleaning cloths, and controlled access to the polishes and other cleaning supplies that you use. She also needs a way to reach areas where she most wants to help, such as the kitchen sink.

Remember that whereas adults do their chores without thinking about the process, children need to have complex tasks broken down into small steps. While your child is learning a skill, you need to ritualize these steps, making sure that everything is done using the same equipment each time and in the same order. Children learn by practice and repetition. Don't be surprised if your child does something over and over for weeks or months until she has mastered the skill.

Of course, it is not the aim to turn your child into a little slave. Sometimes she will be anxious to help; at other times she will be engrossed in another activity. The draw is usually her desire for your attention and approval. Your child will probably not want to go off on her own to accomplish a task. Instead, she is more likely to follow you around and help with the job in which you are engaged. If you approach things without impatience, criticism, or redoing her work because it is not quite perfect, she will delight in helping you to care for her home.

STEP-BY-STEP   Sweeping up

Brooms are irresistible to young children. This simple activity, broken down into careful steps, teaches a skill that will be used time after time as they help clear up after their activities.

One
A taped square on the kitchen floor gives Catherine a target towards which she can sweep debris.

Two
Having learned how to hold her broom with both hands, she carefully sweeps the bits into the square.

Three
To finish, Catherine uses a dust pan and brush to pick up the sweepings. She holds the dust pan level and gets up carefully, watching it all the time as she carries it to the rubbish bin.

Clean and dry
Eden carefully dries the dishes after dinner and takes pride in helping his parents.

IN PRACTICE Your little helpers

Taking careful steps to show children how to achieve grown-up tasks helps them become useful members of the household and develop a sense of self-worth.

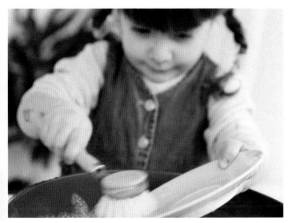

Fun with water
Lily-Rose loves to do the washing up – it is as much fun as water play but with real responsibility and real results.

Shoe shining
Polishing shoes gives Luc a sense of achievement that stays with him whenever he looks down at his feet.

Dustbuster
Using the feather duster to help with the housework is one of Fred's favourite activities.

Learning to pour

Trusting a young child to pour her own drink is unthinkable to many parents, but once again, this is a skill that can be broken down into steps and taught through enjoyable practice. Learning to pour liquids is much easier to master if you give your child small jugs with handles that are the right size for her little hands, and which are not too heavy for her to control when they are full. The entire process is also made easier if as a first step you teach your child how to pour something dry,

such as uncooked rice or lentils, from one small jug to another. For this first exercise, very small jugs such as those used for cream are the best size. Choosing sturdy china or glass rather than plastic encourages your child to be more careful with what she is using. It is a good idea to put a coloured tray under the jugs, then any spilled rice or lentils will be contained and can be easily seen and cleaned up when your child has finished practising. Show your child how to grasp the handle of the jug using whichever hand she is most

STEP-BY-STEP **Pouring from small jugs**

Carefully pouring drinks is a delight for small children. This activity, using two small jugs and some rice or lentils, helps your child to perfect her technique before she moves on to liquids.

One
Lily-Rose practises pouring lentils from one jug to another. A coloured tray catches any that spill.

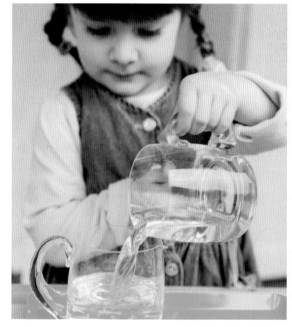

Two
Supporting the jug with both hands, Lily-Rose then practises using water instead of lentils.

comfortable with. Then demonstrate how to support the jug just under the spout with her other hand. This gives her maximum control as she pours. The exercise is to pour the dry rice or lentils from one jug into the other. Then she repeats the process with the other jug. Emphasize the importance of being careful. "See if you can pour the rice from one jug to the other without spilling a single grain."

When your child has mastered this task, you can make it more challenging by giving her slightly larger jugs, and then by having her try to pour the rice into a glass. You can make it more likely that she will succeed by just the right amount of rice into the jug that the glass will hold. Finally, when you think your child is ready, use water instead of dried rice in the jug. Now you can challenge her to pour the water into the glass without spilling a single drop.

Remember, this process is not learnt in a day. It takes most young children many months of practice to gain the hand–eye coordination needed to pour correctly without any help.

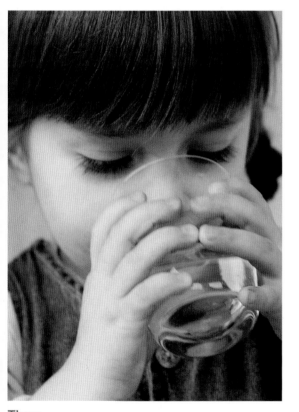

Three
Lily-Rose is now able to pour water carefully without spilling and can pour herself a drink whenever she is thirsty.

SPOONING FOOD

While all of us try to teach our children good table manners, part of the process involves helping them to gain enough fine muscle control so that they are at least physically capable of getting food from a plate to their mouths without dropping it.

Trying some practice games with bowls, spoons, and forks will help to develop mealtime skills. Start with a tray and two bowls, one of which contains something fairly easy to spoon, such as dried butter beans. You will need a spoon that is the right size for your child. Show her how to transfer the beans, one at a time, from one bowl to the other. Challenge your child to do it herself. When she has finished, she can repeat the process as many times as she wants.

Once she can do this without spilling, increase the level of difficulty by replacing the large butter beans with something more challenging, such as dried rice. Repeat the process.

You can use the same process for teaching your child to use a fork if you select the right substances to transfer, such as cubes of cheese or cooked green peas.

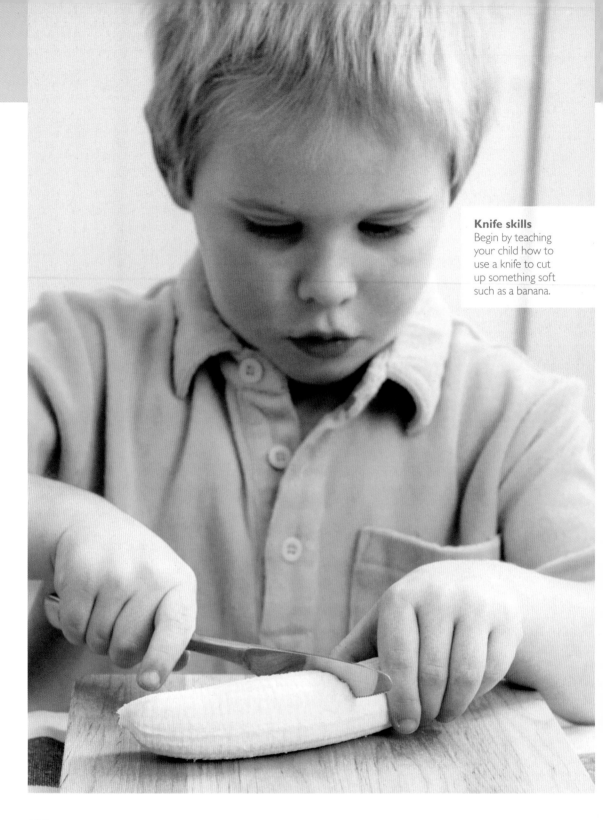

Knife skills
Begin by teaching
your child how to
use a knife to cut
up something soft
such as a banana.

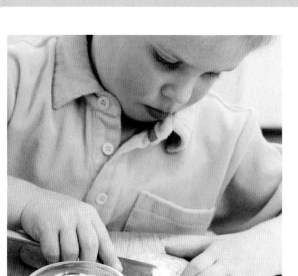

Snack attack
Tom knows where to find his ingredients and a small board and has been shown how to spread cream cheese on a cracker to make a snack.

Ready to go
Tom has learned how to pour from his own little jug of juice. Now his snack is complete.

Preparing a snack

One way to encourage your child to eat healthy snacks is to get him involved in making them himself. Begin by teaching your child how to use a small knife. Choose one that has a rounded point, such as a small cheese knife. This type of knife has an edge just sharp enough to cut through soft cheese or a banana. Show your child how to grip the handle correctly and how to use it to spread butter, jam, and such like on a cracker.

Once he has mastered spreading, you can go on to teach your child how to use the knife to cut up soft food, such as a banana. As he gets older, stronger and more able to control the knife, give him more difficult things to slice, such as apple, carrots, and celery. Within a short time he will be putting these skills to good use helping you to prepare salads and vegetables for dinner.

Make sure your child can find all the ingredients and utensils he needs to make a snack without help by keeping them on a low shelf in the kitchen. Items that need to be stored in the fridge should be kept on a low shelf comfortably within his reach.

Once your child is confident about preparing a snack for himself, encourage him to offer the food to everyone in the family or to visiting playmates. He can prepare a larger plate of sliced banana and some crackers spread with butter or cream cheese and offer his guests toothpicks or small forks, which can be used to lift the slices of banana from the plate.

4

keeping
the peace

create a
loving climate

We can help our children to learn good behaviour, courtesy, and compassion by demonstration, reassurance, and unconditional love.

In a Montessori-inspired home, parents try to be empathetic and caring, respecting children as real and separate human beings. Children also need to develop a sense of empathy for others, and must learn the rules of courteous everyday behaviour.

To accomplish this, we need to help them learn self-respect as well as compassion and respect for others. Since we cannot always be with them, we need to teach them to act with honour and integrity whether or not someone is watching. We can't prepare them for every situation that they will face over the years, but we can teach them how to apply general rules of kind behaviour to new situations.

Baby behaviour

Babies and toddlers don't respond to discipline, rules and punishments, but they do respond to unconditional love. They are not yet at a stage where they know right from wrong. They live in the moment, and when they want something, they want it "right now".

Making an impression
Cuddling your baby releases a chemical cascade of happy hormones in his brain that contribute to his well-being.

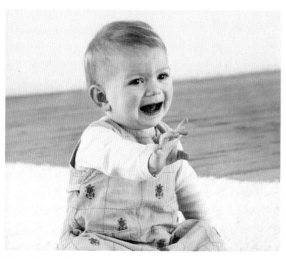

Early learning
You will learn to recognize different cries as
your baby communicates different emotions,
and find the best ways to respond to them.

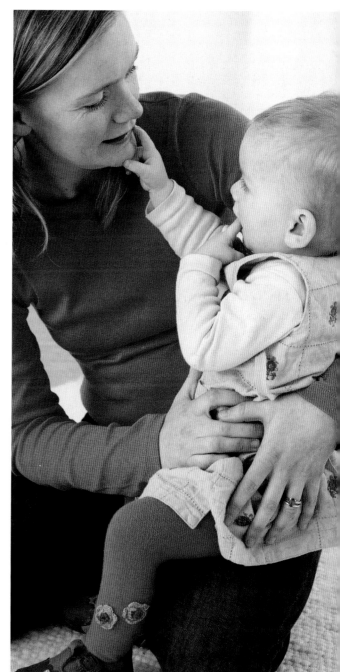

One secret of living happily with very young
children is to work hard at understanding what they
are trying to communicate when they cry. Crying
is one of the few ways they can communicate. It
can mean that they are hungry or that they need
to be winded, they may be in an uncomfortable
position, or they may need a nappy change.

Remember, babies are people too. They can
become frightened. They may be bored or lonely.
They can have bad dreams. Watch and listen
carefully. If you pay attention to your child, ultimately
you will be able to determine what she is trying to
tell you. The behaviour of babies and toddlers is
impulse driven and they have a limited ability even
to make the choice to follow ground rules. While
you always want to model good behaviour and
explain why a given behaviour is acceptable, or not,
don't be surprised when your words go unheeded.

In a climate of love and respect, toddlers develop the ability to understand our words and will begin consciously to respond to them. Eventually, they imitate our actions when we model polite behaviour and will begin to cooperate. Most toddlers have good days when they are cooperative and even angelic, and not so good days where they seem to be testing us constantly.

Teaching older children

Our children love us with a profound affection and want us to be pleased with them. Our aim is to take our children beyond simple obedience,

where they do what we ask in hope of a reward or to avoid something unpleasant. Ultimately, we want to help them to develop an internalized sense of polite, caring behaviour and a clear understanding of what is right and wrong. This requires that children develop a social conscience and a sense of self-discipline, which can only happen as they mature.

Children have the same emotions as adults, but they don't instinctively know how to express frustration and anger appropriately, nor do they automatically know how to solve conflicts. As parents, we have to teach our children how to

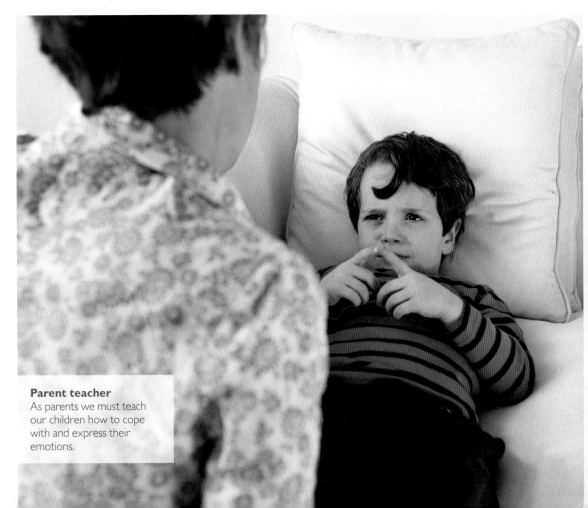

Parent teacher
As parents we must teach our children how to cope with and express their emotions.

"It's better to teach your child the right way to act than to wait for him to misbehave, then scold, threaten, or punish him."

get along with other people so that they are kind and courteous even when we aren't present. For better or worse, all parents are moral educators. Our goal is to show our children the values we hold dear, and to teach them in such a way that they live by them. Children who achieve this develop a high level of self-respect. They also tend to find it easier to establish strong friendships. They respect the rights of others and are generally pleasant people to be around.

As your child gets older, don't take it for granted that he will automatically know how to handle a new situation. It is always better to teach him the right way to act than to wait for him to misbehave and then scold, threaten, or punish him. If your child does act inappropriately, stop his misbehaviour calmly, but firmly, then show him how to handle the situation in a socially acceptable way.

The importance of respect

Some parents and teachers believe that they can shape a child's personality and future through strict discipline, but children carry within themselves the key to their own development. Their early attempts to express their individuality are hesitant and tentative. Our goal should be to help our children to become mature, independent, and responsible. Unfortunately, as parents, we sometimes overprotect our children, not realizing that they can only learn about life through experience, just as we did.

We want to help our children learn to live in peace and harmony with themselves, with all people and with the environment. We work to create a home in which they can learn to function as independent, thinking people. To succeed, we need to treat them with respect as full and complete human beings, who happen to be in our care. Our children need to feel that it is fine to be themselves. If they believe that they are not living up to our expectations or that we are disappointed in the people that they are becoming, then there is a good chance that their lives will be emotionally scarred.

YOUR CHILD'S
BRAIN

A recent study of US preschoolers revealed a strong correlation between permissive parenting and poor self-control in young children. However, researchers found that, to a lesser extent, extremely authoritarian parents also tended to produce children who struggled with self-regulation.

finding a common
parenting style

When a couple become parents, they may have only the vaguest idea of what each partner will expect of family life.

Studies show that children do best if parenting styles are consistent, and, within them, a child feels safe, loved, and can depend on household expectations.

In general, there are three parenting styles: very strict, permissive, and balanced. I favour a balanced approach in which rules and responses are logical and consistent. We set limits, but we want our children to feel heard and to develop a family culture based on some fundamental ground rules of kindness and courtesy. We also model the behaviour we would like to see in our children, so when parents disagree, they need to consider their approach.

Acts of sabotage include openly disagreeing with your partner in front of your child or telling the child in private that you disagree. The better plan is to support your partner while something is taking place, then talk about your differences later.

Taking parenting classes early on; reading and discussing books about childcare is a good way to end up on the same page. Note situations that come up, or that might come up, and discuss how you will deal with them consistently as a family. If you cannot agree, or encounter situations that you feel you cannot handle because they are too dangerous or too upsetting, seek professional help.

> "Children do best if parenting styles are consistent, and, within them, a child feels safe."

Share your approach

Many grandparents play an important role in their grandchildren's lives, helping them to see that there are people who love and care about them beyond their parents. Make sure grandparents understand your parenting style and the need for consistency, but keep your expectations reasonable.

In harmony
Children feel secure when parents work together to find the best way to approach their family life.

coping with family change

We may not be able to control life-changing events but we can manage and mediate their effects on our children.

Predictable routines and care from people who know and understand them form the backdrop to most children's lives, but sometimes the world turns upside down. Events such as the birth of a new brother or sister, or an adoption, bring with them daily upheavals and a confusing mix of emotions for a young child. Stressful times, for example when parents face separation or divorce, or there is a death within the immediate or extended family, can be shocking and traumatic.

Careful handling

Change, any change, can be unsettling to young children. They may or may not be able to express their feelings, but we as parents can try very hard amidst our own sense of excitement, confusion, or turmoil to help our children get through change as gracefully as possible. How do we do this? It depends on your children's ages and, of course, it varies with the situation. There are plenty of self-help books that offer advice on helping children

cope with separation or divorce, and still others that address others forms of loss such as the death of a person who is deeply loved. A key piece of advice in the case of death in the family is to not offer more information than children can handle. Listen to their questions and concerns, answer them as simply as you can, and reassure them that you are there to keep them safe.

In the case of separation and divorce, the same advice holds, but one crucial element is to avoid in any way asking your children to take sides or get in the middle of a conflict between their parents.

"Listen to your children's questions and concerns and answer them as simply as you can."

This is a time to maintain your best grown-up behaviour and do everything possible to be calm and present for your children. Once again, do not overload them with information, and no matter how awful you feel, do not look to your children to comfort you – that is not their role.

Family meetings

The types of situations that can arise in families are legion, but asked to recommend one strategy that can help with most of them, I would say family meetings. These should be a part of regular family life, held weekly among all members from at least age three and up (including grandparents if they live with you). Younger children can simply sit in to absorb the general impression. Provide them with toys or something to do. Keep meetings short at about 10 to 15 minutes, depending on the age of your children. Here are some guidelines.

• Family meeting time is sacred so make sure all family members attend if at all possible.

• Meetings should not be at meal times.

• Turn off all other types of communication; no texting, email, phone calls, computers, or tablets.

• Share the leadership and let everyone take turns leading the meeting.

• Start with thanks and acknowledgments of good deeds and good work.

• Base the first few meetings on fun topics. Later on, difficult topics will be brought to the meeting by the children or by you as parents.

• Family meetings should end with something fun – perhaps a joke, a poem, or a song.

Once established, meetings are valued and welcomed, and become a safe place for you to address anything you face together as a family.

Holding on
When life presents unexpected challenges, a child's security and well-being are key considerations.

sidestepping
tantrums

During tantrums, both children and parents can get completely out of control – but one of you has to be the grown-up.

Temper tantrums are typical among toddlers, although some children carry them on for many years if they find they are a way of getting what they want. Children most commonly throw a tantrum because they are extremely tired, irritably hungry, emotionally overwhelmed, or feeling sick. As your child becomes more "knowing", tantrums may be no more than her way of testing the limits or seeing how you will react.

Children always pick the worst possible times to throw tantrums. You may be driving your car, out shopping, eating at a restaurant or at a friend's

> "A tantrum may be your child's way of testing the limits to see how you will react."

house, and just when you would least expect your child to make a scene, she does. Our tendency is to want to do something right away to get her to stop. We are embarrassed and our stress level soars. This is when parents often resort to threats and punishments. Instead, we need to remember that the tantrum means something, and the only thing that works is to get to the bottom of it and try to address our child's needs.

Types of tantrum

There is a real difference between a temper tantrum in a child who is tired, hungry, or sick, and one thrown by a child who is angry, frustrated, and testing the limits. The first type of tantrum requires little more than a parent determining the cause, remaining calm and upbeat, and helping with food and rest, reassurance and comfort. While it can be embarrassing to have a child crying uncontrollably in a supermarket or on a social outing, at least there is a physical situation

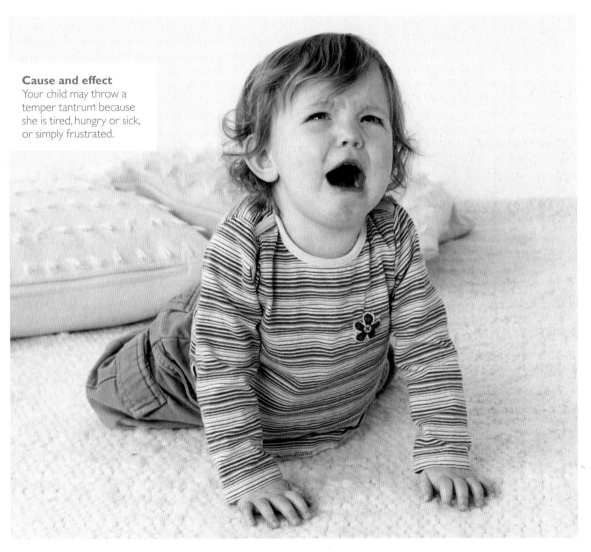

Cause and effect
Your child may throw a temper tantrum because she is tired, hungry or sick, or simply frustrated.

underlying the tantrum that can be resolved quickly once you figure it out. If you do your best to be in control, eventually you will be.

The second type of tantrum is like any power struggle. It is your child's less than articulate way of trying to assert some control in a situation where she feels powerless. Remember, whenever children say "No!" or have a temper tantrum, they are trying to communicate something to you. You have to stay calm, step back, and try to determine what the hidden message is. It might be that all that's needed is for you to listen. Just like adults, children sometimes feel frustrated because they don't feel that anyone is listening to them.

You choose
Avoid power struggles by giving your child choices. For example, choose two outfits you are happy for her to wear then ask her to choose the one she prefers – this way she still feels she has some control.

Resolving issues

It may be difficult sometimes to know for sure what a temper tantrum is all about because young children are not capable of explaining the problem. However, most parents learn to recognize symptoms and can make an educated guess.

If you believe your child's behaviour is a result of her being hungry, find some food for her to eat as soon as possible, even if it's not her usual mealtime. It is always a good idea to carry some sort of healthy snack with you for just such emergencies.

If you believe that your child is overly tired, minimize your talking and speak in a soothing voice, hold or rock her, and take her to her bedroom or some place where she can rest as soon as possible.

If you believe that your child is ill, speak in a soothing voice, quietly reassuring her. If you think she is going to be sick, see if someone nearby can get you an empty bowl or rubbish bin and a warm facecloth. If she needs medical attention, make the arrangements as calmly as possible.

If you have been otherwise engaged, talking to a friend for a long time at the lunch table or on the phone, make sure you give your toddler plenty of attention when you have finished.

Some children have a hard time with transitions, and this in itself can lead to a tantrum. For example, if you are at the playground, let your child know in advance that you will be leaving soon. "We'll have to go home in 10 minutes. Would you like to go down the slide again or go on the swing?" The reminder in advance and the choice will help your child to manage transitions more smoothly.

If your child is clearly testing the limits, stay calm and avoid getting into an argument. Speak in a soothing voice, gently letting her know that while you understand that she is angry, this is still the rule. For example, "I know that you really wish that you could stay here at the playground, but we have to get home to make lunch."

Avoiding pitfalls

Often there are patterns in family life. See if you can identify any regular triggers for tantrums, then try to avoid them. For example, if your child tends to have tantrums when you go shopping, leave her with your partner or with a sitter.

Children often play up when plans change abruptly, and if this is the case with your child, talk plans through in advance and stick to them.

Explain the limits to your child before you do something. For example, if you are going shopping and your child wants to buy a toy, tell her in advance what you will agree to and stick with it. Do not give in to children's attempts to get you to back down, whether they are whining, demanding, or attempting to manipulate the situation. Distracting a toddler with a game at the first sign of a tantrum

can work. However, if she does not calm down, disengage by sitting down to read or stepping just outside the door, letting her know you are waiting to offer a cuddle as soon as she is ready.

Many families try to do too much. Toddlers prefer routines and get angry and tired when swept along from one activity to the next. Sometimes it is unavoidable, but think long and hard before you sign your child up for baby gym, dance lessons, or any other prescheduled classes. Racing from one activity to another raises everyone's stress levels and sets the stage for temper tantrums.

YOUR CHILD'S
BRAIN

Difficult situations trigger the stress response in a child, increasing heart rate, blood pressure, and the release of the stress hormone cortisol. If the child is supported throughout by a caring adult, the effects are buffered, helping a healthy stress response system to develop.

COPING TIPS

There are several things that you should remember when your child is having a tantrum:

• Don't resort to violence by slapping or spanking your child. That is the surest way to teach her to be violent to others.

• Don't try to restrain your child physically in the midst of a temper tantrum, unless she is about to run out into traffic or harm herself in some other very real and immediate way.

• Don't resort to threats or punishments. When children are being irrational, these simply don't work and only escalate the emotional turmoil already begun.

• Don't argue. You can't win a debate with someone who is being irrational!

• Don't try to embarrass your child or ridicule her behaviour. This teaches her to lash out at other people in the future.

• Don't attempt to deal with a temper tantrum in public. Take your child to somewhere you can be alone and talk in private. This is courteous to others and makes it easier for you to handle the situation.

Banishing bedtime battles

Bedtime can either be a special time or turn into a power struggle between parents and children. Children can resist going to sleep for many reasons: they resent being told they have to; they are afraid that they will miss something; they are not tired; or they simply want to remain close to their parents. As in any situation, ask yourself what your child's behaviour is really trying to tell you. Then look for a way to give your child some of what she wants, and still get her to go to bed.

Establish a routine

A good bedtime routine might include a bedtime snack, followed by a bath, brushing of teeth, reading a story, then a snuggle before tucking your child in and kissing her goodnight. Do the same thing every evening; bedtime rituals help children calm down and feel reassured. Begin your bedtime ritual an hour or so before you actually hope to have your child asleep. Keep everything calm. This is not the time to do

> "Do the same thing every evening – bedtime rituals help children to calm down and feel reassured."

anything to encourage excitement. Give a warning 10 minutes or so before it will be time to begin the ritual. This allows your child time to wind up whatever activities she is engaged in. Try to avoid power struggles by offering your child choices, each of which is acceptable in your eyes. For example, "Would you like Mummy or Daddy to tuck you in tonight?".

If your child has difficulty going to sleep, try using guided visualization, a process where you use words to describe a pleasant, calming experience. Some parents like to use soothing music in the background. You might tell a gentle story, such as how you and your child are going on a trip by magic carpet or sailing down a beautiful river.

Another strategy is to have a conversation with your child about happy memories. "Do you remember when you were little and I used to carry you on my shoulders?" Or you might tell each other something that you particularly appreciate about one another: "I love the way you are so kind to everyone. It makes me really proud to be your Mum." Encourage your child to talk about her day by asking the right questions, for example, "What was the best thing about today?" rather than "What did you do today?", which usually prompts the answer "Nothing".

YOUR CHILD'S
BRAIN

Sleep has a profound effect on children's ability to learn. A team of German and Swiss researchers have shown that material that children learn subconsciously during the day is transformed into active knowledge in their brains during long periods of deep sleep overnight. The process is much more effective in children than in adults.

Once your bedtime ritual is over, leave your child's bedroom quietly. To avoid the endless pattern of your child getting up and coming to find you, tell her in advance that "Except for a real emergency, if you come to find me after you've gone to bed, I will gently take you back to your room". Don't get into a debate, and don't give in. Be calm, gentle and consistent. If you are inconsistent your child will bend the rules more and more to see if they still hold true. Sometimes the rules have to be set aside to respond to something important that is going on with your child. For example, she may wake up in the middle of the night because she is frightened or sick. Follow your instincts.

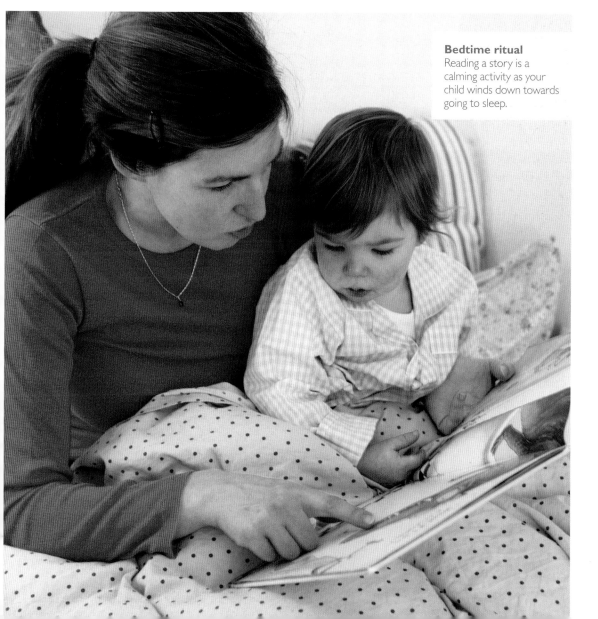

Bedtime ritual
Reading a story is a calming activity as your child winds down towards going to sleep.

a positive approach
to discipline

Many parents believe that the word discipline means
to punish. In reality, it means to teach.

Every child will test the rules to some degree. In
fact most acts of testing parents are a normal part
of a child's process of growing up. When children
test adults, it is often their way of expressing
feelings that they don't understand, and from our
responses they gradually learn how to handle their
emotions appropriately. By testing the limits, they
learn that we really care about certain ground
rules of grace and courtesy in our relationships. In
acting out, they are taking their first tentative steps
towards independence, attempting to demonstrate
that we don't control them completely.

Family ground rules

It is my impression that some families have far too
many rules, when all that is needed are some basic
guidelines that underpin what we expect and hope
from all members of the human race. There is
no need to be creative and think up something to
govern every aspect of your children's lives. Agree
on your family ground rules and get them written
down and displayed where both parents can
refer to them. Teach your child how to do the right
thing rather than focusing on his mistakes. In the
Montessori-inspired home there are usually just
a few basic rules.

• Treat everyone with respect.
• If you use something, put it back correctly
when you are finished.
• If you break or spill something, clean it up.
• Tell the truth and don't be afraid to admit when
you make a mistake.

You should be absolutely clear in your mind
about your family ground rules. Explain them
positively, rather than as prohibitions. Instead
of saying "Don't do that!" the rules should tell
your child what he should do. Teach him how
to follow them as if you were teaching any
lesson in everyday life skills. Model the same
behaviours that you are trying to encourage in your
child. Consciously try to catch your child doing
something right and reinforce and acknowledge

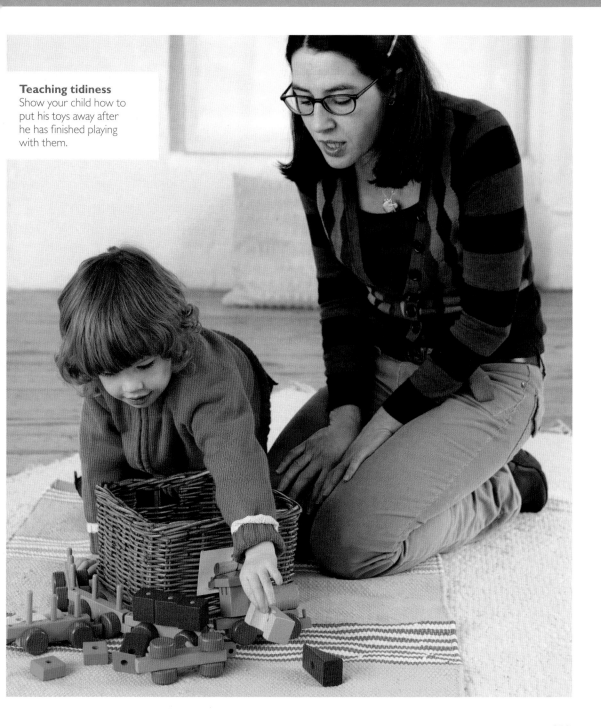

Teaching tidiness
Show your child how to put his toys away after he has finished playing with them.

even the small steps he is taking in the right direction. Don't wait until he has mastered a new skill – encourage him along the way.

When your child is breaking a ground rule, there are several things you can do other than scold, threaten, or punish. You can redirect him by suggesting a more appropriate choice. You can remind him of the ground rule and politely but firmly ask him to stop. If the situation is not emotionally charged (that is, if you are not personally aggravated), you can re-teach the basic lesson about how to handle such situations.

Broken rules

If one of your ground rules is no climbing on the furniture yet you find your children bouncing on the sofa, politely but firmly ask them to stop, then remind them of the rule and why you have it.

Be consistent. If you find that you cannot bring yourself to reinforce a rule again and again, it shouldn't be a ground rule. A few good rules are much better than dozens that are often ignored.

Cut down on the word "no"

Sooner or later, every child will stubbornly say "No, I don't want to!" This is the power struggle that starts in the toddler years and often continues throughout childhood and adolescence. Many people call the toddler stage the "terrible twos" but they don't have to be – not with two year olds or with older children (see panel, right).

Power struggles get going in situations where parents and children are each determined to get their own way, and neither party is willing to back down. Underneath, each feels frustrated and threatened. Parents feel that their children are directly challenging their authority. Children in situations such as this are usually feeling powerless, and are attempting to assert their autonomy and establish more of a balance of power in their relationship with their parents.

Don't punish, teach

Threats and punishments are not good tools to get children to behave. When children are angry, or are asserting their independence, they often misbehave and don't care if they are punished. Those children who do respond to threats and are shaken by punishments are anxious to please us and win back our love. Arguably, these children will respond just as well to other forms of discipline. While punishments tend to produce immediate results, they are rarely long-lasting and work only if the person being threatened cares.

Teach your child to do things correctly and emphasize the positive rather than using insults and anger. Above all else, try never to ask your child unanswerable questions, such as, "How many times do I have to tell you?" to which the appropriate response would be, "I don't know, Dad! How many times do you have to tell me?".

"NO" STRATEGIES

Here are some strategies to help reduce the number of power struggles and use of the word "No!"

• Give your children choices. Whenever you can, look for ways to let your children make a choice between two equally acceptable alternatives. "Would you like to have water or milk with your dinner?"

• Teach your child to say "no" politely: "Mum, I really do not feel like doing that now."

• Keep in mind Robert Heinlein's golden rule of family life: "Kindness and courtesy are even more important between husbands and wives, and parents and children, than between total strangers."

• Don't simply give in – look for ways that might allow you to back down gracefully. Often, through compromise, both you and your children can get most, if not all, of what you are after.

• Power struggles can be minimized by giving your child meaningful levels of independence and responsibility in everyday life. This makes her feel powerful and grown up.

• Reserve "no" for the really important issues such as an activity that might harm your child or others, or cause damage.

understanding
your child's
personality

By recognizing, accommodating, and celebrating our children's different personalities, we show that the world welcomes them as individuals.

When you were young, were you the child who ran into school, excited to be there, or were you hesitant? Were you the most popular one in class, or often alone? Did you enjoy team sports from an early age or prefer to read a book? Perhaps one of the hardest things for us to recognize as parents is

> "Perhaps one of the hardest things for us to recognize as parents is that our children are not ourselves."

that our children are not ourselves. You may be surprised at the distinct differences between your personality and your child's, or maybe your child's behaviour reminds you of something in your own personality that you wish you could change. Each of us is unique: parent, child, grandparent. We have different interests, temperaments, and abilities, and each of us sees the world and interacts with others somewhat differently. Children benefit from discovering this basic fact – and so do parents.

Temperament and personality

Your baby comes into the world with an underlying temperament. You may have a cranky infant who wails pitifully in unfamiliar arms, a sleepyhead, or a gregarious baby who smiles and coos at everyone. Even in babyhood, a one-size-fits-all approach to

Sharing the fun
Open-hearted personalities
are usually gregarious and generous.
An extrovert preschooler is often a
wonderful playmate for younger
siblings and friends.

parenting will not work. As babies become toddlers, temperament evolves into behaviour traits. Your toddler may be shy, cautious, and defensive, often absorbed in his own activities and hesitant about new experiences. Easy-going, even-tempered types adapt more readily to most situations, while high-spirited toddlers tend to dive in head first. If you regularly "watch and follow your child" (see pages 48–49) you will soon develop a good understanding.

The shy child

The introverts of this world may suffer more than most, and this can be especially true in childhood. We have all seen the despairing mother at a party pushing her daughter into games, or the dad in the playground urging his timid son to the top of a climbing frame. If instead, we acknowledge and validate how a child is feeling, it sends the message to a child that it is fine to be who he is: "I know you don't like those horses on the carousel, Jack. When you are bigger you might want to have a go."

When a situation might be taxing for a child, lay the ground with quiet conversations. "We are going to a party for Grandad's 70th birthday. Your cousins and aunts and uncles will be there, and people and children that you don't know. When we sing Happy Birthday, where do you want us to be?"

Remember, too, that sometimes children will surprise us with a response that we would have not predicted. A typical example is the child who is

HOW PERSONALITY DEVELOPS

The way that temperament develops into a set of personality traits is dependent on a number of factors in the early years.

• A child needs a warm, loving relationship with those around her.

• She needs to grow up with clear guidelines that enable her to develop self-control and feel confident about her actions.

• She should be given an environment that is rich in opportunities for exploring and following her passions and interests.

• Her first teachers should tailor their educational approach to her strengths and interests and help her overcome the things that she finds difficult.

• She needs to be acknowledged and valued as an individual and also encouraged to be part of a group.

• She needs regular affirmation that it is just fine to be the way she is.

Sunny personality
A child with a sunny temperament receives plenty of warm attention and is often happy to be centre stage.

hesitant with strangers and new situations, but goes off to Montessori school, and after a day cannot wait to get back to school each morning.

Challenging behaviour

What do we mean by challenging behaviour? It pushes our buttons? It is particularly serious? Nothing is working and we've tried all the usual things? The first question to ask is whether this is normal behaviour for the age. Toddlers have limited attention spans, poor social skills, and are inclined to throw things and explore beyond the limits of their own safety. Managing their behaviour is often a matter of managing your own expectations: avoiding high-end restaurants, monitoring situations that trigger tantrums (see page 121), offering a boisterous toddler opportunities to let off steam, and finding quiet corners in busy places for a nervous child.

Is it common behaviour when you consider the situation? When there is a new baby in the house attention for the older child is often in short supply. "That's a beautiful new baby sister," a Grandma told her truculent grandson. "But now I want to read a story to someone who can talk to me."

When all the relatives are at our house for a celebration or a family reunion, we may briefly see unrecognizable traits in an excited group of overstimulated children, and we make allowances.

That said, some children seem to pitch headlong into every situation, and there are times when it feels as if they are beyond control. Such a child needs regular reminders of the ground rules: you may not hurt or endanger yourself, other people or living things, nor may you deliberately damage the environment, whether your own belongings or

Watching and waiting
For many children, shyness is a natural response to new situations. The imminent arrival of a new sibling can affect confidence too.

others. This child needs to be offered outdoor activity in all kinds of weather, and plenty of interesting pursuits indoors.

Challenging children often come to expect negative reactions, so notice and reward good words and deeds. Remember that children change as they grow, and what you find challenging when they are young may develop into positive characteristics as they get older. Children amaze us because they are people right from the start. Sometimes we forget.

teaching lessons in grace and courtesy

Practising with games that teach good manners can help your child learn how to behave well in any company.

Few people seem to consider the value of teaching children the fine details of acceptable behaviour. In Montessori schools the "lessons in grace and courtesy" – exercises which set a tone of respect and kindness – sit alongside the more conventional subjects on the curriculum. We show our children how to shake hands, greet a friend and say goodbye. We demonstrate how to interrupt someone who is busy and how to tell someone "no, thank you" politely. We teach children how to speak indoors and how to play nicely. We show them how to offer a sincere apology and how to resolve conflicts peacefully.

Simple lessons

The first step is to explain a situation in simple terms and demonstrate the right way to handle it. Then have your child practise with you, role-playing the sequence of events. Children enjoy these lessons so long as they are kept short, and if they have not been embarrassed or threatened for making a mistake.

For example, if your child tends to yell at the top of her lungs inside the house, you need to show her how to keep the noise to a level that does not disturb other people. First, as it is happening, instead of scolding, politely but firmly ask your child to speak softly please. Then, choose a moment when neither of you are upset about the behaviour to give her the lesson on the right way to speak indoors. Speak in simple language and show her what you mean. For example, you might say: "I want to talk to you about indoor voices. When we are outdoors, it's so big, and sometimes we need to shout so we can

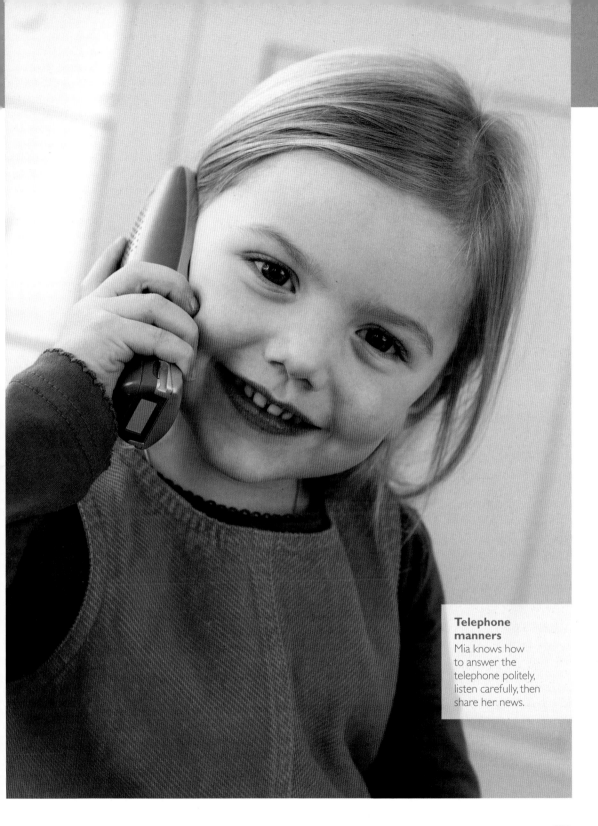

Telephone manners
Mia knows how to answer the telephone politely, listen carefully, then share her news.

hear each other. Outdoors, it doesn't hurt our ears when someone talks loudly. So, outdoors we can use our outdoor voices. But when we are indoors, it hurts our ears and bothers the neighbours if we talk too loud. When we are indoors, we need to remember to use our indoor voices."

Now show your child what you mean. Talk very loud, and ask, "Was I using my indoor voice or my outdoor voice?". Talk normally. "What do you think? Was I using my indoor or my outdoor voice? Indoors, we use our indoor voices. Outdoors, we use our outdoor voices."

You can teach all sorts of lessons this way, everything from saying "please" and "thank you" to closing doors without slamming. Some families have the manner of the week. They introduce a new rule of everyday courtesy each week, and practise it with one another over meals and generally around the house.

Role models

To teach children good manners, they need to see that their parents, older siblings, and friends follow them consistently as well. The example that we set through our own behaviour is more powerful than anything we say. Children are absorbing everything they see us do, especially when they are very young, and soon they begin to talk and act just like us. We are their role models.

Bearing in mind that your child will be influenced profoundly by the people around her, choose wisely the children and adults with whom she will spend time. Avoid loud, chaotic situations where large groups of children are over-stimulated and generally behave rudely.

Choose your child's playmates thoughtfully. If she spends time with a family that allows children to create havoc in their home, don't be surprised when your child brings that behaviour home with her. Pay attention to the way prospective playmate's parents supervise their children. Do they ignore them or talk on the phone amidst chaos? It is not your place to judge other families and how they behave, but it is your obligation to make good choices for your child.

COURTESY LESSONS

Here are some more ideas for lessons in grace and courtesy:

• saying "please" and "thank you"

• using a kind tone when speaking: no whining or yelling

• how to ask for a turn or if you can play too

• how to introduce yourself

• how to open and close doors

• what to do if you have to cough or sneeze

• giving people compliments and encouragement

• allowing others to pass in front of you or to go first

• saying "excuse me" if you bump into someone

• responding politely when someone calls you or says your name

• walking around areas where other children are working or playing on the floor and not stepping over them

• learning how to wait

• not interrupting other people when they are talking

• answering the telephone politely

IN PRACTICE Learning kindness, courtesy, and manners

Children learn by example but can also be shown how to behave in a caring way using role play. Present these short exercises in calm moments rather than using them to point out a mistake.

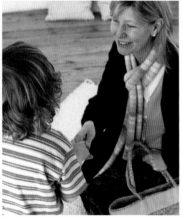

Meet and greet
Teach your child the correct way to welcome visitors into his home.

Care and compassion
Encourage your child to show concern for a friend who is upset.

Table manners
Your child can learn to pull a chair out and put it back, and how to sit down on it correctly.

Coordination and control
Practising walking carefully along a line, watching where she is going, teaches your child balance and coordination.

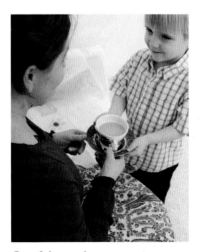

Careful carrying
Teach your child how to bring something to you, carrying it using both hands, and then to set it down correctly.

Saying goodbye
Your child starts to learn friendship skills when she is shown how to offer warm greetings and goodbyes.

solving problems at
the peace table

When children need help to resolve issues, directing them to the peace table can help them find words to settle their differences.

From time to time, children fall out with siblings or friends – it may be over something as simple as whose turn it is to play with a toy or over a bigger issue such as friendships. Sometimes they reach the point where they are too angry to reason with each other. This is where the peace table comes in: it provides a place where the children can cool off as they follow a procedure that stops the argument in its tracks.

The peace table is usually a child-sized table with two chairs, a bell, and a flower or ornament that symbolizes peace, perhaps a rose, an olive twig, or a dove. If you're short of space, two chairs together are fine or a rug in the corner of a room or even a particular spot on the stairs. When children are accustomed to the ritual they may decide to go to the peace table without being prompted; at other times a parent or older sibling may see a row developing and suggest the participants try to solve their problem at the peace table.

Once at the table, a certain procedure ensues. The child who feels especially wronged places one hand on the table and her other hand on her heart, indicating that she speaks the truth, from the heart. She then looks at the other child, speaks her name and explains how she feels about what has occurred and how she would like the disagreement to be settled.

The second child then has a turn and the dialogue continues until an agreement is reached. If the children cannot manage this themselves, they may need a mediator – maybe an older sibling or a parent. If the problem is too involved, they may ask for a family meeting, where the whole family listens to both sides of the story.

What children learn from the peace table is that regardless of their size, age, or position in the family, their point of view will be heard and they can expect to be treated fairly. The core experience they gain from these procedures is that arguments need to be settled with honesty and goodwill to maintain a harmonious, cooperative atmosphere at home.

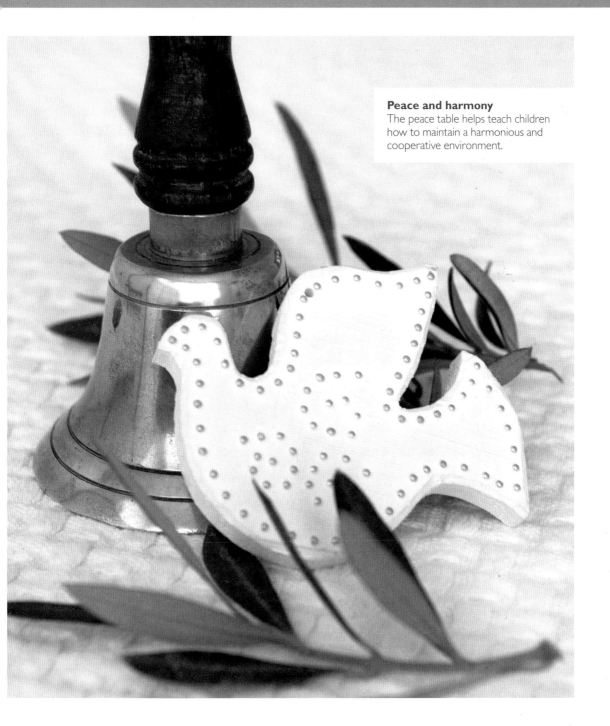

Peace and harmony
The peace table helps teach children how to maintain a harmonious and cooperative environment.

STEP-BY-STEP ## Making peace

The peace table could be regarded as the polar opposite of a "naughty step". It helps children to cool off, calm down, and settle their differences in a much more positive way.

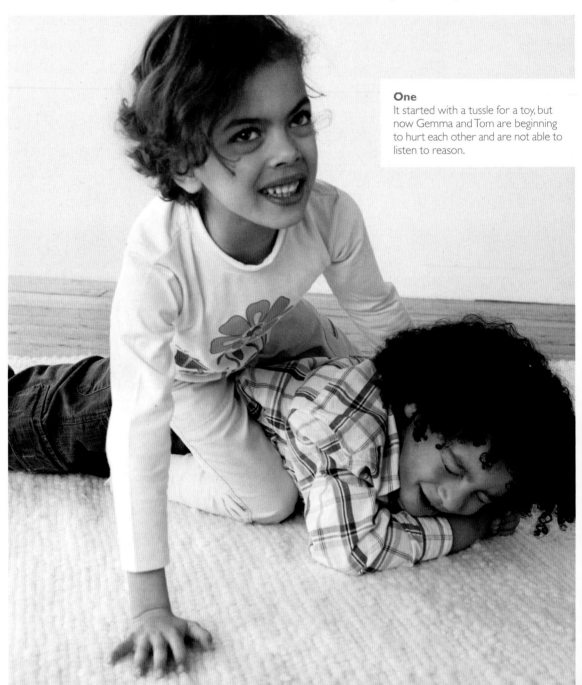

One
It started with a tussle for a toy, but now Gemma and Tom are beginning to hurt each other and are not able to listen to reason.

Two

In an effort to resolve their dispute, Gemma and Tom are encouraged to break off from fighting and each take a seat at the peace table.

Three

Tom puts one hand on the peace table and his other hand on his heart and calmly explains to Gemma what it is about her behaviour that is upsetting him.

Four

Gemma now proceeds in the same way, placing one hand on the table and the other on her heart, and responds to what Tom has said.

Five

When both Gemma and Tom feel that the differences between them are resolved, they ring a bell together to let the rest of the family know.

taking control of
the television

Television is a major source of conflict in many households. Establish some family ground rules regarding viewing, then stick to them.

Children's values and knowledge about the world have traditionally been shaped by four cultural influences: home, school, religious organizations, and peer groups. Today, television represents a fifth and incredibly powerful culture over which most of us have scant knowledge and exercise little control. This is unfortunate, especially when you consider that it has become the babysitter of choice in all too many families.

Passive parents

There are several problems with uncontrolled television and children. The violence portrayed is of great concern. In one year a child might see thousands of murders, fights, car crashes, and mid-air explosions. Certainly, the values and problem-solving approaches considered appropriate by many producers differ from our own.

An even greater concern is the hypnotic character of television viewing. Many parents observe that their young children can sit for hours enthralled by Saturday morning television. Of course, they sit and watch for long periods: they are effectively in a trance. Television viewing is at best a passive experience. It requires no thought, no imagination, and no effort. Quality children's programming can be terrific, but most of what's available is anything but.

Making rules

Television is best doled out carefully in planned and measured doses. Children really do not need television to entertain themselves. Establish some

"Television is best doled out in measured doses; you can limit the number of hours per day."

family ground rules that make sense to you. Determine the shows that you are happy for your children to watch, and limit the number of hours a day you allow your children to spend in front of the set. Give your children as much choice as possible: "You can choose from among the following programmes; however, you can only watch three of them in any one day. What do you want today's choices to be?"

Some parents consider whether or not commercial television shows are appropriate on a case-by-case basis. Select those with an educational element, but limit the amount of time in any one day that your children spend watching them. Sometimes a programme may have real value, but it may have confusing or disturbing content. In these cases, the whole family should watch it and then discuss the issues it raises together once it has finished.

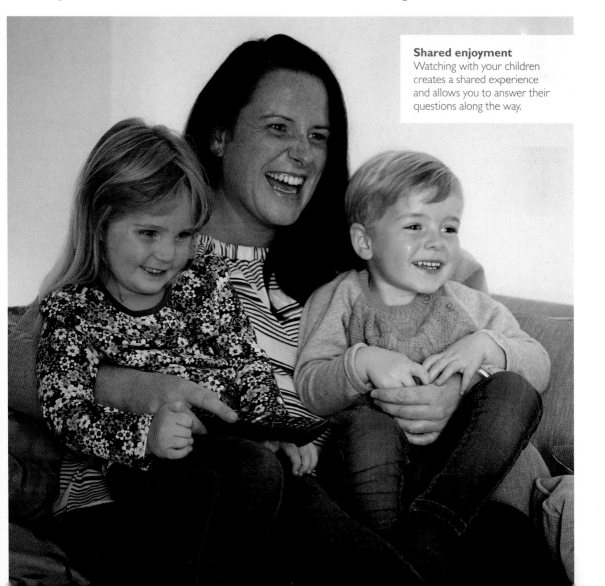

Shared enjoyment
Watching with your children creates a shared experience and allows you to answer their questions along the way.

managing
screen time

Devices and apps have been developed to such a state of simplicity that even the youngest children can access them at the touch of a fingertip.

SMART USES

Choosing apps that support your child's real-life activities and interests will make her first forays into the digital world meaningful and appropriate.

• Show your child the picture icon and let her browse a small library of memory photos of family members and holidays. Allow her to take her own smartphone pictures on discovery walks.

• Include your child in a video–chat session with distant friends and relatives.

• Follow up a favourite story, or one of those many questions about how something works in the world, with a quick search for a video clip. "Here's how baby polar bears play on the ice."

• Install some apps with simple matching games and puzzles that have attractive images.

• Show her how to find and play her favourite songs.

• Make up funny stories together and record them to play back on long car journeys.

All around us we see babies in pushchairs swiping screens, and school-age children absorbed in their individual digital devices, and wonder whether face-to-face communication and long attention spans are endangered human qualities. Where this is leading is of some concern to those of us who believe strongly that babies and preschoolers need to start out with concrete experiences that feed their development. We know that we can offer hands-on activities that will excite their interest in the world around them without the need for smart devices.

Role models

Our children's first role models are ourselves, and they copy us slavishly from their earliest days. It is unsurprising, then, that your baby abandons her toy to haul herself up to reach the sleek, touch-screen phone that seems to occupy her mum's every waking minute. Keep a check on your own use of digital technology at home. Are smartphones and tablets appearing at the dinner table? Is your attention constantly hijacked by every email or text that pops up? Do you read or watch television with a tablet on your lap? A study in US schools revealed that students who are addicted to their devices struggle to comprehend texts that previous generations found easy. We need to be sure we are not modelling an attention deficit for our children.

With thought, we can apply our principles of offering meaningful activity in a controlled way to devices. When your child is at least four or five, introduce a robust smartphone or tablet with a careful, step-by-step demonstration. Set up activities that turn the device into a tool of discovery rather than a passive plaything, and give your child the autonomy to browse and choose as she pleases, keeping within firm time limits each day.

YOUR CHILD'S
BRAIN

In one of the longest-running studies of human health, development, and behaviour, researchers in Dunedin, New Zealand, have followed more than 1,000 children from birth in the early 1970s. In the first eight years of the study, children were given regular tests to measure their ability to pay attention. When subjects were reviewed again as adults at the age of 32, a good concentration span in the early years was shown to be the strongest predictor of future success.

Online vigilance
Monitor what children explore online and impose parental controls. Bookmark sites with well-researched content and images.

5

exploring the wider world

children are
little scientists

Children have an inbuilt drive for discovery. Encourage your child to observe the world and to feel a sense of wonder.

Maria Montessori believed that all children behave like "little scientists" in that they are eager to observe and make "what if" discoveries about their world. Babies and toddlers test the environment to see what happens when, for example, they drop a toy out of their highchair or play with the water in their bath. This drive for discovery continues to develop as they grow and become more adventurous in the things that they try out, from making mudpies in the garden to starting a worm farm. Children are born with marvellous imaginations and a keen desire to explore the world. Encourage this in your child – help him to discover the beauty and wonder of everything around him.

Child's-eye view

Remember that your child's world is up close and low to the ground. Seeing life from his point of view can help you to rediscover the sense of wonder of a young child. Keep in mind the slow-moving pace of his world. Follow your child's lead, and be prepared to stop and examine anything that captures his interest – a ladybird or a flower, for example. Don't get impatient when he dawdles – give yourself time to adjust to his pace.

The best way for children to learn is by doing things, not by being told about them. This is especially true when they are young, but it also applies to older children and even adults. When children are young, they are not only learning things, they are learning how to learn. No book using words and illustrations to describe the world

> "See the world as your child sees it – up close and low to the ground."

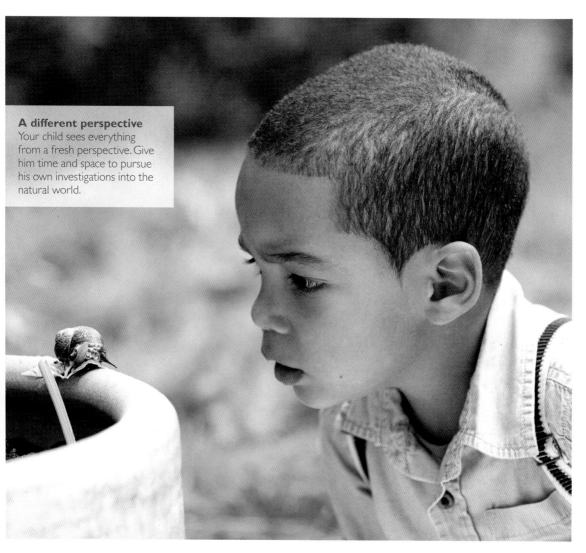

A different perspective
Your child sees everything from a fresh perspective. Give him time and space to pursue his own investigations into the natural world.

that exists around a small brook or under a rotting log can replace the value of spending time closely studying the real thing. Books and other materials help children to pull these powerful impressions and experiences together in their minds, but the foundation needs to be laid in direct observation and hands-on experience.

The outdoor world

Children love to be outdoors, wandering around, climbing trees, picking berries, collecting conkers. They enjoy helping to look after the family garden or feeding small animals such as ducks, rabbits and chickens. They form life-long memories of days spent hiking with their parents in the woods,

147

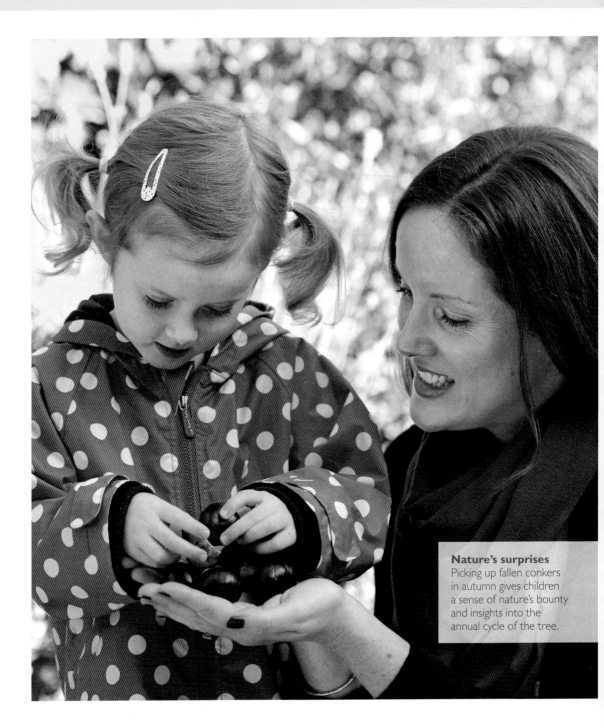

Nature's surprises
Picking up fallen conkers in autumn gives children a sense of nature's bounty and insights into the annual cycle of the tree.

playing in a creek, discovering sea creatures in rock pools, and walking along a beach looking for shells, driftwood, and pebbles.

You will probably begin your child's life outdoors by taking her out for little excursions in her pushchair or carrying her on your back. Take time to introduce her to your world. Even very young babies absorb the sights and sounds of the outdoors – clouds passing overhead, the sight and smell of flowers in the garden, the wind rustling the leaves in the trees. All these leave a strong and lasting impression. Whether it is summer, autumn, spring, or winter, every season has its own beauty. Point out small things: a tiny flower poking up through the snow, a beautiful shell, bright berries, a perfect leaf.

As your child gets older, begin to point out familiar things as you walk around. "Look, there's Grandma's house! What lovely flowers she has growing outside her door!" or "My goodness, Mary, can you see the nest those birds have built in the tree? Some day they will lay eggs, and they will have baby birds up there!" In the winter, when you see animal tracks in the fresh snow, ask who might have been walking there.

Stewards of the planet

Another key Montessori idea is that children are stewards of the Earth and must learn to care for distant places such as rainforests and ice caps as well as rural places and pockets of nature within the city or suburbs, and to preserve them for the future. Teach your child a reverence for life. After all, we are all part of the web of life, dependent on the delicate balance within the natural world for our own existence. For example, children often learn to think of the soil as "dirt", a word that implies something nasty to many people. Teach them to respect good, rich soil and all the life that it supports on our planet.

Emphasize the need to treat every living thing with care. Teach your child not to pick leaves and flowers aimlessly then toss them aside, but to gather them only for a good purpose. It is fine occasionally to gather wild flowers, then dry or press them or place them in a vase with water to preserve them for as long as possible, but never over-pick any one plant or flower. Teach your child to walk gently upon the Earth, taking only what she needs.

Encourage your child to enjoy the forest and meadows, leaving nothing behind. Teach her never to litter. If you see litter on the ground, pick it up and carry it with you until it can be thrown away. This is especially true of bottles, broken glass, cans, and plastic bags, which are not only unsightly but also could harm animals. To gather up cans and broken glass safely, you might carry an old canvas shoulder bag. As your child gets older, give her a bag of her own to collect litter in, too.

YOUR CHILD'S
BRAIN

US researchers have found that young children who spend time regularly outdoors, engaged in activities such as hiking and camping, are more likely to become adults who care about the environment than children who grow up with little contact with nature.

working in the family garden

Helping in the garden is a great way to build practical skills and to feed your child's quest for discovery.

When you plan your garden, try to make a space where your child is free to experiment and grow things. From an early age, children can be involved in the cycle of the year, from planting seeds indoors or in a cold frame in the early spring and transplanting the seedlings to the garden when the danger of frost is past, to tending the garden and watching the fruits and vegetables grow, all the way to harvest. For young children, there is something marvellous about going out into the garden and bringing in a basket of lettuce, spring onions, and tomatoes that they helped to grow – I've found that getting children to eat vegetables is rarely a problem when they have grown, picked, and washed them themselves.

Don't forget to include fragrant herbs in your garden. The aroma of fresh basil, fennel, and sage should be part of your child's memories of childhood. The fact that they can be picked and eaten, adding colour, scent, and flavour to your food, is yet another benefit.

> "Getting children to eat vegetables is rarely a problem when they have grown them themselves."

Child-sized equipment

You can buy garden tools, watering cans, and wheelbarrows that are just the right size for your child. Set up racks in your garage or garden shed to hold these special tools, and teach your child to clean them and return them to their places when she is finished for the day. Provide child-sized gardening gloves and sturdy dark green gardening aprons to help teach your child the concept of neatness and order. Look for child-sized baskets to hold the flowers, fruits, and vegetables that your child collects from the garden as they become ripe and ready to eat.

When space is limited

If you don't have a family garden, consider window boxes or create a container garden. With the right soil, watering, and a sunny location, you can raise an amazing amount of produce in a small space – strawberries, tomatoes, peppers, beans, and herbs are all easy and convenient to grow. One of the greatest advantages of container gardening is that it puts the garden at exactly the right level for small children.

Flower power

Leave space in your garden for flowers, both wild flowers native to your region and the traditional annuals and perennials that add beauty to our gardens and grace our tables. Teach your child how to pick them and arrange them in little vases in the house. Young children often prefer to put one special flower in a very small vase, rather than create large arrangements. You can use the nicely shaped bottles in which individual servings of drinks such as Perrier and Orangina are sold.

Keep your child's flower-arranging kit on a low shelf within her reach. As well as a variety of small containers for her to use, you will also need a small pair of garden scissors to cut the

Budding gardener
Planting bulbs is rewarding for small children. Show your child how to check plants to see if they need to be watered.

Autumn tidy up
In chilly weather, children enjoy having energetic tasks such as raking up leaves.

flowers, a small jug to use for adding the water, a funnel to make it easier to pour water into the openings of small vases and a sponge for cleaning up. You might even want to include some small doilies to place under the vases.

Flower arrangements allow your child to bring nature inside your home – they add to the beauty of your rooms, as well as deepening your child's awareness of different plants and flowers.

Garden vocabulary

Teach your child the correct names of each flower, fruit, and vegetable as they come into season. Before you know it, she will be able to name everything in your garden. You can also teach her the adjectives that describe them: red, large, small, long, rough, silky, and so on. Many plants also have practical uses in cooking and around the house. Aloe, as one example, is a wonderful ointment for scrapes and burns.

Hang beautiful pictures of plants and flowers in your home, both close-up art photographs and prints of famous paintings. Your child's library collection should include some of the many enticing books about flowers, animals, and the natural world that have been published. Many children enjoy finding pictures of flowers or leaves they have found in their gardens in the pages of their books.

Crafts from nature

Don't forget that all sorts of crafts use flowers, leaves, seeds, and grasses. Children love making art with natural materials. They can learn to use a small flower-press to preserve leaves and flowers, and mount them in scrapbooks. They can weave with grasses and make little pine-needle baskets. Acorns and pine cones can be used for all sorts of crafts, such as making table decorations; and the branches of many hardwood trees that have pleasing bark can be used to make bark rubbings and nature collages.

ANIMAL VALUES

There is no better way to encourage your child to appreciate living things than to invite some to become members of your family. Family pets help to instill compassion and a sense of responsibility. Even a small child can wash a pet's bowl and fill it with food, while older children can be taught how to clean out pens and cages, or take the dog out for walks. If your home allows, consider the possibility of some small farm animals, such as rabbits or chickens, in addition to the more traditional cats and dogs.

Animals are our fellow travellers on this Earth. Where once people believed that human beings had the right to dominate nature, many of us now understand that we are interdependent with all of the world's plants and animals. Animals deserve kindness and protection from cruelty, and such attitudes begin within your family.

going for a walk in
the forest

Make walks in countryside or parkland, exploring
nature, a regular feature of your family life.

You can make walks exciting by adding a goal –
set your children the task of collecting samples
of something specific, such as different types of
flowers, leaves, rocks, or grasses. Each child can
carry a small paper bag for their specimens. Explain
that a specimen is a sample of something that you
find interesting or want to know more about. You
may want to put a limit on how many samples each
child may collect (three to five items at most).
A mobile phone camera is handy for taking pictures
of passing animals and birds, interesting bark and
fungi, and spiders in webs.

When you are out walking be sure to talk to
your children about what they are experiencing. Talk
about the weather and the seasons. What do they
notice? What does the sky look like? Is it sunny? Are
there clouds? Point out other things that they might
not notice, such as the colours of leaves on the trees
and other seasonal clues. As you walk, encourage
them to remain quiet at times so they can hear the
sounds of nature as well as observing.

Don't be deterred by bad weather – it does
children no harm to feel the sensation of rain
or wind on their faces. Children can be expected
to walk a mile for every year of their age, so
don't underestimate their capabilities. Stopping
for snacks or a picnic gives them time to recharge
as well as to sit down and observe and enjoy the
outdoor world around them.

Preserving nature

Once you are back home, empty the contents of
your specimen bags onto a plastic garden bag and
ask your children to tell you what each item is.
Is it living or non-living? Where did they find it?
What do they know about it? On other occasions,
make the weather, birdlife, or forest sounds the
focus of your walk, and take pictures and jot
down what your children see and hear in a
notebook. Explain that if people always collected
specimens from nature, eventually there would be
nothing left for other people to enjoy.

Off the beaten track
Away from the pathways, children can clamber on logs, paddle in small streams, and enjoy the feeling of rustling leaves and squishy mud underfoot.

IN PRACTICE **Outdoor activities**

Walk in all weathers. Following a familiar route in your local park or countryside gives children an understanding of the seasons and insights into the changes they bring.

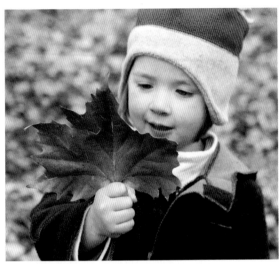

Leafy lessons
Leaves are a great source of seasonal information. Ask your children to describe their shape and texture as well as colour.

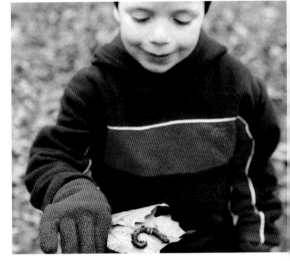

Living creatures
Watching a worm creeping over a leaf will be a source of great interest and entertainment for your little scientist.

Look this way
Show your child how to use binoculars to bird watch. Take a spotter book with you to help him identify what he sees.

Tall stories
Walk at your child's pace, allowing him to stop and absorb what he can see and feel whenever he wants to. Sitting looking up into a tree can provide a different perspective.

Learning to observe
Take time to stop and examine things your children are attracted to when walking. Don't overburden younger children with too much detail about their discoveries – ask them to describe to you what they can see.

WHILE OUT AND ABOUT

Plan out a comfortable circular walk and give yourself extra time for some of the following diversions. Follow a squirrel • adopt a tree • roll in the leaves • sit by a lake and watch the geese • look for wild strawberries • hunt for unusual stones • search for wild flowers (don't pick them – observe, study and remember) • lie on your back with your head up against the trunk of a tree and look up into the branches • listen to the wind • watch birds in their nests • follow a butterfly • study the shadows cast by the sun • learn the names of the trees around your home • study the shapes of leaves • use charcoal and tracing paper to make bark rubbings • collect seeds • look for tiny baby trees • search for pine cones • look for animal tracks • find a fallen tree whose wood has begun to decay – explore what lives there • sit still with your eyes closed • listen to the birds calling • look for baby ferns • smell the breezes • find a little glen where fairies might like to live • have a picnic outside in a meadow • run down a hill with your hands spread wide like an aeroplane • float popcorn boats down the stream • take a bag and pick up litter along the path • look for fungi – but don't touch or eat them.

make your own
nature museum

When your child brings specimens home, help him to create his own nature area where he can observe and learn.

Most children have a strong desire to bring some samples of nature home with them and will be delighted if you can find ways to accommodate their finds. Depending on the space you have available, a nature area in your child's room can be anything from a simple table of "finds" and snapshots of outdoor discoveries, to an aquarium and terrarium housing the worms, bugs, beetles, frogs, and other small animals that he has found and invited back for a short stay.

> "Older children enjoy photographing and drawing nature, from sweeping landscapes to an isolated flower…"

In our home, we called our nature museum the Dew Drop Inn. In the spring and early summer we had small flowerpots holding wild flowers and baby trees that we found in the nearby woods. We brought caterpillars back to keep in a covered terrarium so that we could see the chrysalises that formed and the moths or butterflies that emerged. We collected frogs' spawn and watched them turn into tadpoles before releasing them in the pond near our house. From time to time, we even hatched baby chicks in an incubator. And, of course, the occasional litter of kittens or puppies was the highlight of any year.

Our children studied flowers, comparing different species and counting petals and stamens. In the autumn, they collected fruits, nuts, and berries, noticing how they were distributed and which animals looked at them as food. They brought specimens back to the nature museum for identification, labelling, and display. They also collected and pressed flowers and leaves, mounting them onto cardboard or into small, bound scrapbooks. On small shelves, the children displayed collections of their finds: abandoned birds' nests and eggs, snake skins, tree sections and samples of bark, cocoons, mounted insects, and preserved animal bones.

Tightly covered terrariums and aquariums provided homes for the ants, chameleons, newts, lake bass, and turtles that came to visit our house for a while. Root boxes – planters with one wall of glass so roots can be seen growing – were a big hit.

Small beginnings

Gather together some basic items to get your child started: a magnifying glass or lens, a simple microscope, bug boxes and jars, guidebooks for identification, cards for labelling, and scrapbooks. As his interest grows, you may want to add more sophisticated equipment such as an ant farm, root boxes, a terrarium, an aquarium, and an incubator. Install bird feeders and nesting boxes outside. You can now buy commercial butterfly kits that supply chrysalises to your home at the right time of year.

As your child gets older, he may like to keep a journal of his observations at home and in the field. Encourage him to write poems and stories that capture the sense of wonder and beauty all around him. Older children often enjoy drawing and photographing nature, from sweeping landscapes to an isolated flower, leaf, feather, or fircone that has been carried home to the nature shelf.

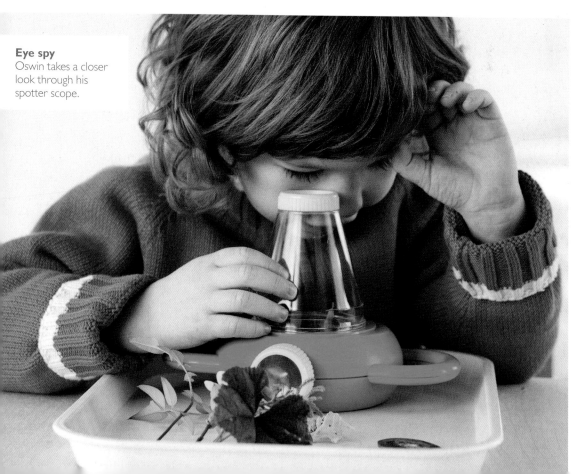

Eye spy
Oswin takes a closer look through his spotter scope.

playing nature-based
party games

There are many great games for parties or groups of children that teach them about the world. Here are three of them.

When you have large groups of children over for special occasions such as birthday parties, play games that will teach them about some aspect of their world while also keeping them entertained.

The waterhole game

This game is played by eight or more children – you might want to play in the garden rather than risk getting your carpets wet! Tell the children that they are going to pretend to be animals, such as antelope, coming down to the waterhole at night to drink. One child is a predator, such as a mountain lion. He sits in the middle of a large circle, surrounded by cups of water. He is wearing a blindfold and is "armed" with a spray bottle of water. One by one, the antelope creep up to take a drink: picking up a cup of water and carrying it back to their seats. The lion cannot see them and depends on his hearing. If he hears an antelope approach, he can spring once, shooting a spray of water in the direction of the sound. If a child

is splashed, he or she must leave the group. As soon as every antelope has taken a drink or has been "caught", the game is over.

The food chain game

This is a variation of the game of tag, and is designed to teach children the basic concepts of a simple food chain. Choose a food chain with four levels and describe it to the group of children. For example, plants are eaten by grasshoppers, which in turn are eaten by frogs, which in turn are eaten by hawks completing the food chain.

• Divide the children into three groups. In a group of ten, have seven grasshoppers, two frogs, and one hawk.

• Give each child who is pretending to be a grasshopper a small plastic bag, which represents the tiny tummy of a grasshopper. Tie a strip of wide brown ribbon on the arm of each grasshopper.

• Give each child who is pretending to be a frog a bigger bag representing a frog's larger tummy.

Predator and prey
The mountain lion sits quietly, waiting to catch the antelope in the waterhole game.

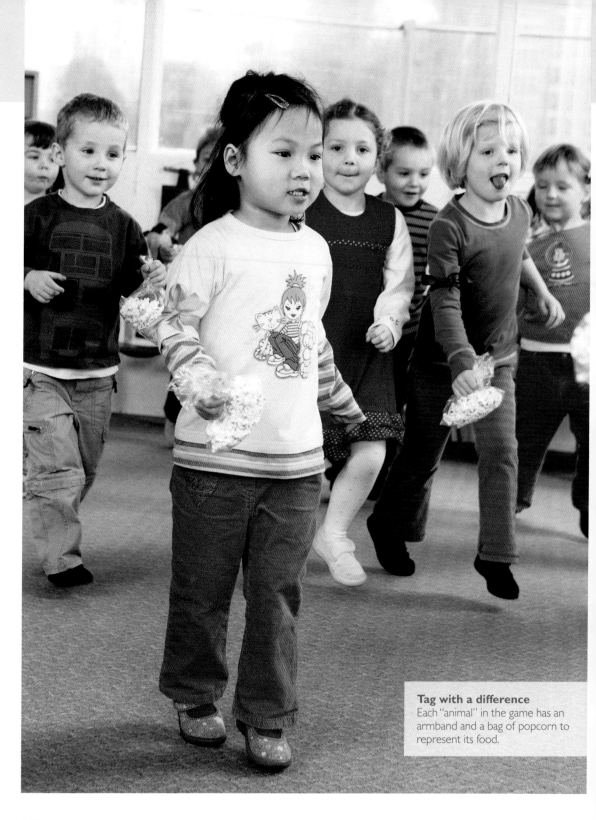

Tag with a difference
Each "animal" in the game has an armband and a bag of popcorn to represent its food.

Now tie a strip of wide orange ribbon on the arm of each frog.

• Give a large plastic bag to the child who is pretending to be a hawk. This represents the still larger tummy of a hawk. Tie a strip of wide green ribbon on the arm of the hawk.

• Now spread a thin layer of popcorn across the carpet or lawn to represent the plant food for the grasshoppers. Explain to the grasshoppers how they "eat" the popcorn by stooping down to pick it up one piece at a time and putting it in their plastic bags. Set the frogs chasing the grasshoppers and if they catch one, they can empty the popcorn from the grasshopper's tummy (plastic bag) into their own tummy and that grasshopper sits out. Set the hawk to chase the frogs and again if he catches one he can empty the contents of the frog's tummy into

his own and that frog sits out. After five minutes, see how many grasshoppers and frogs are still in the game and have survived the food chain.

The web of life game

This is a good rainy day activity that can be played with ten or more children. You will need a selection of stuffed toy animals or pictures of animals to represent the various animals in the web of life – a bird, a worm, a frog, a turtle, a fish, a bee, a cow and whatever other familiar creatures you wish to include. You will also need pictures of a tree, grass, a flower, and the ocean to represent water. In addition, you will need long strands of different-coloured string.

Invite all the children to sit down in a large circle. Ask "Who will be the Sun? The Sun sits here in the middle of our circle." The child who sits in the middle wears something yellow to represent the Sun. "Now what plant or animal would you like to be, Olivia? Oh, the wolf! Good. Here you take the toy wolf and hold it in your lap." When each child has picked a plant, bird, or other animal, take each in turn. "Who needs the Sun? Do birds need the Sun? Yes, they do!" "Who needs water? Do birds need water? Yes. Do elephants need water? Yes, they do!"

As you connect each plant or animal to whatever it needs, run a piece of string between the two. This builds the web of life, which, when you are finished, is very complex and beautiful. "See, we all need one another!"

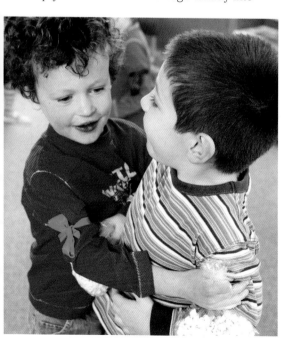

Top of the food chain
The hawk in a green armband seizes a passing frog and captures his bag of popcorn.

making cultures
come alive

Introducing our children to different cultures helps cultivate their sense of wonder and curiosity as well as dispelling prejudice.

All of humanity is part of a global family. We share the same needs, and have more things in common than divide us. Today, most communities reflect a tapestry of people from a wide range of ethnic and cultural backgrounds. Our role as parents is to encourage our children to live in peace and harmony with all people. Prejudice is not inborn; it is acquired, and our first duty is to help ensure that our children grow up open-minded and comfortable in our diverse societies by modelling warm and positive interactions with people of every culture. We can do this by introducing them to people from different cultures and ethnic backgrounds, by fostering positive opinions and ideas, and also by exploring and experiencing the cultures of different countries.

Cultural studies

To learn of far away places, to dream, to imagine, to hope to go there some day has always allowed children and adults to embrace the whole world

and to care about its well-being. I can think of no educational objective that is more important. In Montessori schools, cultural studies take children beyond acceptance to understanding, appreciation, and celebration of different cultures and countries. To accomplish our goal, we have to make things that are foreign to children's experience come alive. Montessori schools make use of multi-sensory, hands-on experiences and international celebrations drawn from all over the world. We focus our studies on one given theme or topic at a time, looking at it from many perspectives. For example, when we study Africa, we look at the land itself, the climate, the plants and animals that live there, the people and their housing, food, dress, lifestyles, stories and legends, art, music, traditional dance, and celebrations.

You can use much the same approach at home. Young children are interested in other children and like to hear stories about how children live in other countries. They enjoy trying new artwork, listening to music, and learning songs and folk dances from

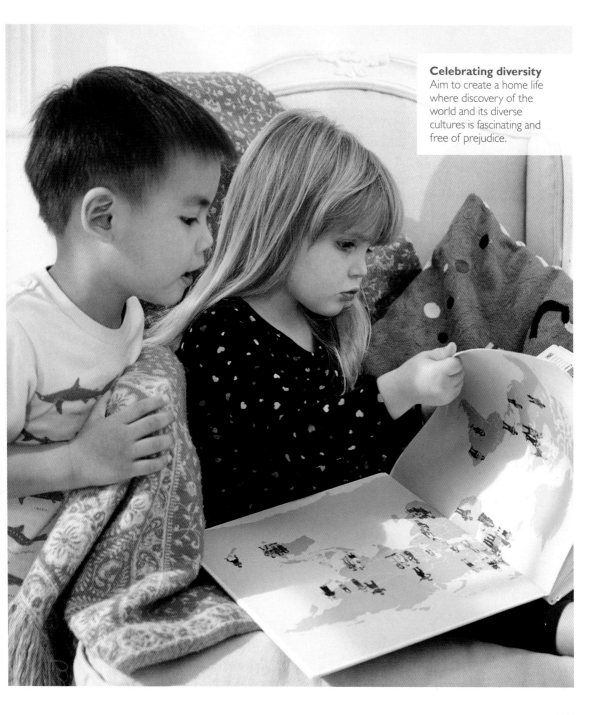

Celebrating diversity
Aim to create a home life where discovery of the world and its diverse cultures is fascinating and free of prejudice.

around the world. Dressing up in different costumes is fun and creates a lasting impression. Exploring foods from different cuisines lends itself to multiple sensorial experiences; most children will try something new if they are also involved in the process of preparing it.

Which culture?

Start small and simple. Just focus on one country for your first year. You might like to start with a lovely picture book or a film about the country.

Simple things such as collecting pictures and postcards are a good early step.

Keep the following points in mind.

• Begin by admitting that you don't know everything about the culture you are studying but, just like your child, you are learning more.

• Convey curiosity and adventure. Pretend that you are all going on a trip to this interesting country, and you are preparing for it.

• Always speak with respect and care about the culture. Children pick up your underlying emotions.

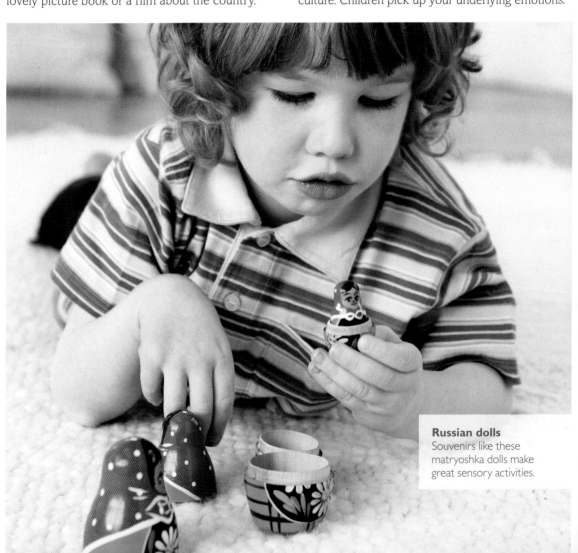

Russian dolls
Souvenirs like these matryoshka dolls make great sensory activities.

• Make sure that everything you share with your child about the culture is authentic and accurate.

• Try out some simple greetings and courtesy phrases in the language of your chosen country and practise them together.

Create a display

Gather as much information as you can about the country you have chosen from the internet and from books. Borrow artefacts from relatives and friends who are from the country or who have been there; some people may be willing to loan you artwork, recordings of foreign music, or authentic native costumes. These can be arranged as a display somewhere in your home for a short time, and then returned.

If you are visiting the country you are interested in, make a collection while you are there. Look for stamps, coins, and paper money; newspapers and magazines; posters and postcards showing cities, landmarks, and everyday scenes, and bus and train tickets, and entry tickets for museums and galleries. crafts such as pottery, baskets, carvings, statuettes, model houses, boats, and dolls dressed in traditional costume. Pick up a traditional hat or piece of a costume for children to try on.

Set up a special area, a table or shelf, somewhere in your home to display your treasures: dolls, toys, artwork, books, model houses, picture collections, coins, and the like. It is useful to have a wall behind your display so you can hang a poster or painting as part of your display. Your children and their friends should find the cultural display attractive and appealing. Decorate it with items such as paper lanterns, sculpture, brightly imprinted fabrics, flags, ornamental fans, and flowers.

CULTURAL HOLIDAYS

Your family will have a number of holidays that you celebrate every year. These would normally be the major religious or cultural holidays that are part of your family's tradition, along with those that are celebrated in the country in which you live. Some common holidays in the United Kingdom include:

• New Year's Day

• Burns Night (Scotland)

• Chinese New Year

• Valentine's Day

• Shrove Tuesday

• St David's Day (Wales)

• Holi (Hindu)

• St Patrick's Day (Ireland and Northern Ireland)

• Mother's Day

• Passover (Jewish)

• Easter (Christian)

• St George's Day (England)

• May Day

• Father's Day

• Eid-al-Fitr (Muslim)

• Rosh Hashana and Yom Kippur (Jewish)

• Diwali (Hindu)

• Hallowe'en

• Guy Fawkes and bonfire night

• Remembrance Day

• Chanukah (Jewish)

• Christmas (Christian)

a Montessori birthday party

Montessori schools use a special celebration that you can easily adopt at home to mark your child's birthday.

Traditional birthday parties often tend to focus on presents, party bags, and lots of sugary food. A Montessori birthday celebration takes a different approach, aiming to introduce a little wider understanding and ceremony into the proceedings. Children are given a first impression of the relationship between Earth and the Sun and taught that a year is the amount of time it takes for Earth to circle the Sun once. Children are also told the story of their lives, year by year, from birth to the present day.

Counting the years

You will need a small globe to represent the Earth, a candle or lamp to represent the Sun, and a circle (or ideally, an ellipse) drawn on the floor with masking tape or laid out with a long piece of yarn, representing the orbit of Earth around the Sun. Make notes about important events in your child's life to date, and collect photos of her at different ages to help tell the story of her life so far.

On the day of your child's birthday, gather your family around the line, leaving plenty of space so the birthday child can walk freely. Bring the candle (or lamp) and the globe to the gathering. Have your notes and the photos ready. Place the candle in the middle of the circle and light it. Remind the children that this flame is fire and is very hot, so they must sit in their places and watch from a distance.

> "A Montessori birthday celebration introduces wider understanding and ceremony into the party proceedings."

STEP-BY-STEP Celebration

In this ceremony, children learn that their age is linked to Earth's journey around the Sun.

One
A candle represents the Sun and a globe represents Earth. A collection of photos tells the story of Mia's first four years.

Two
Mia's mum lights the candle at the centre of the rope circle and explains how Earth takes a year to travel once around the Sun.

Three
Mia carries Earth around the Sun four times. After each circuit Mum describes Mia at that age and hands out some photos.

Four
Mia's friends sing a birthday song, then Mia blows out the candle to mark the end of the ceremony. Now it's time for party food and games.

Say, "This candle (or light) stands for the Sun – the same Sun that we see up in the sky. The Sun is a big ball of fire that keeps on burning and doesn't go out."

Take the globe and walk slowly around the line on the floor, saying: "This globe stands for Earth, the planet we live on. Earth goes around the Sun. It takes a long time for Earth to go around the Sun. Every time Earth goes all the way around the Sun, a whole year has gone by. It takes a year for Earth to go around the Sun one time." Now give the globe to the birthday child and ask her to get ready to walk slowly around the line just as you

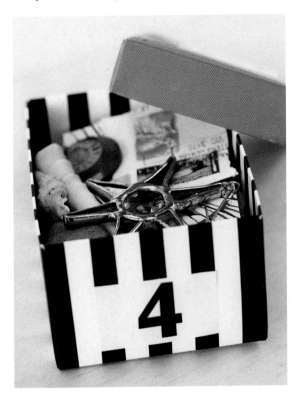

Memory box
Keep your collection of mementos for each year in boxes so your child can look through them and reinforce her memories of herself at different ages.

did. Begin to tell her story, something along these lines: "Today is Mia's birthday, and we are going to celebrate it in our special way. Mia is going to carry the globe and walk slowly around the line four times, because she is four years old.

"Mia is just beginning her journey with Earth around the Sun. She hasn't been born yet. Mummy and Daddy are waiting anxiously for her time to come, and Grandma and Grandpa Willis have come to stay at our house to help when the new baby is born. Mia, would you take one step forward please?" Mia walks forward one step. "Now Mia has been born. She is tiny – only this big – and all pink and wrapped up in a blanket. Mummy and Daddy are so proud. Here is a picture of Mia as a newborn baby.

"Mia, would you walk all the way around the line? Stop when you get back to that spot. Mia is one year old and she is celebrating her first birthday with her family…" Continue the story in this manner. When Mia has walked around the line the correct number of times for her present age, say, "Mia is now four years old, and today is her birthday. The Earth has gone around the Sun four times. Four years have gone by since Mia was born." You may wish to end the celebration by singing a birthday song, then let your child blow out the candle.

Time capsule

Some families like to compile a time capsule of objects to help their children to look back on and remember the year gone by. This might include photos, a copy of some family film footage, a letter from mum and dad, and perhaps some art or other objects that your child decides to add. The box should be kept safe in a place where she can look through it whenever she wishes.

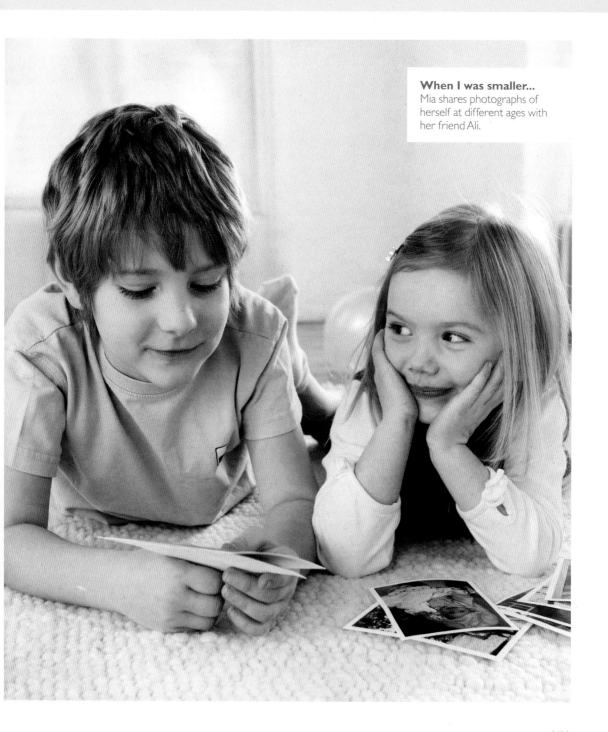

When I was smaller...
Mia shares photographs of herself at different ages with her friend Ali.

6

the best time to learn

the foundations
for learning

The sensitive period for language begins at birth, and all young children respond to an environment that is rich in words.

Some children also enter their sensitive period for learning academic skills at an early age; others will not show the slightest interest until they are older. With the right approach you can increase the odds that your child will want to learn to read, write, and work with numbers with natural enthusiasm. This chapter shows you how to let your child develop at her own pace, within a home environment that provides the right stimulation and support.

PUSHY PARENTS

Learning is not a race. Children learn at their own pace and, in general, it has been observed that the more parents push, the more children resist. Pushy parents see children as an extension of their own status as adults; if they have a child who reads at three, then clearly they have done their job as parents well. But if a child ends up quietly resentful of lessons, teachers, work books, and tests, then what have we really accomplished?

Reading aloud

Most of us provide a wide variety of books for our young children, and this can begin soon after the birth of the first child. Publishers increasingly appreciate the importance of beautifully illustrated children's books, and wonderful selections are available. As my grandmother used to say, "No matter how tight our budget was over the years, we always made money available for good books."

"As soon as your baby is able to sit and focus, spend time together looking at a variety of picture books."

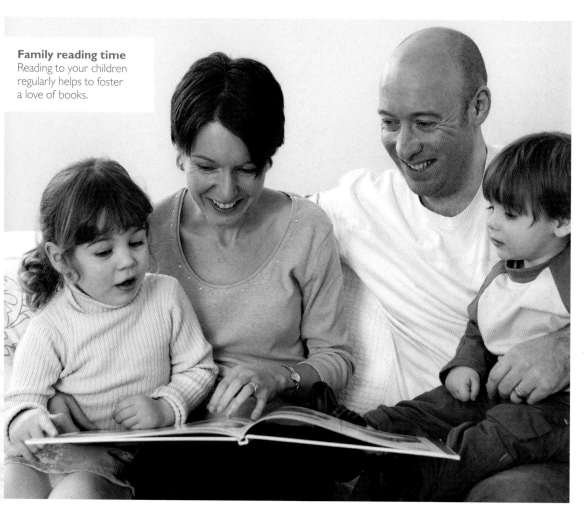

Family reading time
Reading to your children regularly helps to foster a love of books.

As soon as your baby is able to sit and focus, she will enjoy short periods spent on your lap looking at picture books and hearing you talk about what is on the page. As she grows, read to her every day, not only at bedtime, but whenever you can. Pay attention to her favourites and try to maintain your enthusiasm when you are expected to read them over and over again. Children are absorbing those stories into themselves by repetition.

Keep talking

As you care for your baby and toddler, talk about what you are doing. This ties your actions to language, and helps your child to develop an extensive vocabulary. "I am going to change you now. Oh my, were you wet!" or "I am going to pick you up. Here we go. I'm lifting you up high onto my shoulder." Talk about what you see your child doing as it happens: "You must be very thirsty.

Talking together
Speak clearly and precisely
to your child. Her eyes will
tell you whether or not she
has understood everything
that you are saying.

You are drinking so much today." "You dug that hole just right for this flower. Now you can put the flower in the hole." Speak clearly and be very specific in what you say: "Put all of the blue buttons in with the other blue buttons." Although your child may not understand what words mean, there is no need to use baby talk.

It is important, however, not to assume that your child understands you. Use simple words and phrases and look her in the eye as you speak to her. If you watch her eyes, you can usually tell if she understands what you are saying or is confused. Does she look away? Demonstrate your meaning if your child does not seem to understand. As your child's ability to understand grows, the language you use should become more complex in vocabulary and sentence structure. Stretch her with new words. Turn the TV or radio off unless you are watching or listening together – a noisy environment hinders language development.

When your child is very young, help her to communicate without words. Use mime to act out stories or situations. Invite your child to play, too. "Pretend that you are carrying a giant puppy, as big as a horse!" "Pretend that you are a bird

> "When you care for your infant and toddler, talk about what you are doing. This ties your actions to language."

YOUR CHILD'S
BRAIN

Your child's vocabulary matters. A study of UK school children found that, in a group of 100 seven year olds, the highest performing 25 per cent had a vocabulary of around 7,100 root words, compared to a vocabulary of about 3,000 words in the lowest achieving 25 per cent. To catch up in five years, the low-vocabulary group would have to learn three or four new root words every day. Parents' input into a child's vocabulary has been shown to be a major factor, regardless of family background.

flying in the sky. Flap your wings like this!" You can also act out what many words mean (big, tall, fast, slow, smile, sad). Older children continue to enjoy this, too.

Teaching household names

Teach your child the correct names for things around the house. In their sensitive period for language, children can easily absorb new words and grasp their meaning. The more words they learn, the better. Even though your child may make words up or mispronounce them, don't use silly words yourself. Just use the correct name, recognizing that your child's ability to understand and vocalize a complete range of sounds will develop in stages. For example, in the first instance your child learns the word "dog", and learns to distinguish a dog from a cat. From there, you can begin to teach words that further define dogs and cats. Learning that your dog "Biscuit" is a French poodle, and your neighbour's dog "Toby" is a Bassett hound would be one example. Learning the names of familiar animals and birds, flowers and trees, fruits, vegetables, body parts, and things found around your home are all good examples that can be taught using the Montessori three-stage lesson (see opposite page). A large vocabulary is a solid foundation for a lifetime of learning.

Using descriptive words

Once your child knows the words for lots of objects, start to extend her vocabulary by teaching her new words that describe the objects and their location.

THE COMMAND GAME

It may not seem to be the case sometimes, but children love to follow orders in a game. Start with simple one-step commands: "Please give me the toy truck" or "Please give me the truck that is over there." Then make commands more challenging by adding a description of an object and its location. "Would you give me the large red bucket on the top shelf over there?" For young children this gets much more difficult if the object you ask for is in another room. Don't be surprised if they get lost along the way if you try this too soon.

The game can be made more challenging as children get older by adding in more than one step. "Would you please take these flowers to the worktop next to the sink and put them down? Then choose a vase and put about this much water in it. Then put the flowers in the vase and arrange them to make them pretty for the table. When you are finished, put them on the table and we will make it very special for our guests."

You can start with words that describe the colours of objects. Start by introducing the primary colours (red, blue, and yellow), then the secondary colours (green, orange, purple, and so on), and then familiar shades of colours (lilac, rose, pastel blue, tan, and so on).

You can then teach her words that describe colours, such as pale blue, deep pink, bright yellow. You can also introduce your child to words that describe size (big or small, short or tall, thin or wide), taste (salty, sweet, sour), weight (light and heavy), texture (rough and smooth), and so on.

As your child learns the basic descriptive adjectives, begin to introduce her to comparative language: bigger and biggest, longer and longest, taller and tallest. This vocabulary is essential when children are working with the sensory activities described in chapter two. "Which one of these cubes is the largest? Now, which one comes next?"

When your child appears to have a good grasp of descriptive words, ask her to describe things in her own words. "How would you describe Toby (your neighbour's Bassett hound)?" Encourage her to retell stories or to describe what she is doing as you make dinner together.

Enriching vocabulary

Montessori teachers use a three-stage process to help children develop a rich vocabulary. Children learn what words mean when they can associate the name with an object. For example, here's how you might teach a young child the names of secondary colours.

In the first step show your child an orange-coloured paint sample. Name the colour: "This is orange." Now show your child a green-coloured paint

sample. Name its colour: "This is green."
Finally, show your child a purple-coloured paint
sample and say, "This is purple."

In the second step, help your child make a link
between the language and his own experience by
giving him the name of an object and asking him
to find it. "Show me orange." He should point to
the orange sample. Next ask him to "show me
purple" and he should point to the purple sample.
If your child makes a mistake, simply re-teach the
lesson. Returning to the first step, point to the
purple sample and restate, "This is purple." Point
to the green sample and restate, "This is green." In
the third step, we ask children to name something

without naming it first as we did before. Point
to one of the paint samples and ask, "What
colour is this?" Your child should answer,
"orange". If he makes a mistake, re-teach the
lesson by patiently reconfirming the names of
the samples, using the first and second steps.

A broad range of words
To begin with you can use the three-stage
lesson approach to introduce your child to lots
of different everyday objects, such as types of
fruit or vegetables (for example, pepper, artichoke
and butternut squash, as shown below), animals,
birds, and household objects. Repeat the game

STEP-BY-STEP The three-stage lesson

Once you have learned this simple sequence, you can use it in many situations. It is pleasing
because it builds gradually on what the child knows rather than trying to catch him out.

One
Oswin's mum tells him the names
of three different vegetables. She
points to each one as she says
its name.

Two
Now she asks him to point to
one of them – the butternut
squash. She does this for each
vegetable in turn.

Three
His mum then picks up one of the
vegetables and asks Oswin to
tell her its name. He is thrilled to
find that he knows the answer.

179

with the same set of objects over several days or weeks – only move on to a new set of objects when it is clear that your child is confident about remembering the names in the first set.

As your child gets older you can continue to enrich her vocabulary by using the three-stage lesson. Introduce terms from geometry (equilateral triangle, square, cube, pentagon), botany (plant, grass, tree, leaf, stem, lower, petal, stamen) or the various land and water forms that make up our planet's surface (mountain, island, lake, ocean, river, isthmus). The more words children know, the more they observe and try to identify what's around them.

Telling a story

Ask your child to choose an interesting picture in a magazine and to cut it out. Then ask her to tell you something about the characters or animals shown in the picture. Your older child may want to make up a story. Write down what she says, word for word, printing it out neatly or typing it into the computer and printing it out using a large font. If you print just one sentence on each page, with the text at the bottom, your child may like to glue in her picture, then add her own illustrations for the different pages. Print them on nice paper and bind them into a book by punching holes in the paper and tying a ribbon through each hole.

Help your child sign her name on her work when she has finished. If she can't write yet, encourage her to make a mark, or to draw a smiley face, or to write out one letter. She will soon begin to sense the connection between marks written on paper and the spoken word.

Questions and feelings

When your child is ready to talk, be ready to listen. At other times, prompt her by, for example, asking what she thinks will happen next in a story. "How did the baby bear know someone had been sitting in his chair?" "It was broken and someone big must have sat in it." Keep the conversation going by avoiding closed questions that can be answered with a simple "yes" or "no". Open-ended questions help your child to develop her ability to organize and communicate her thoughts out loud. "What would you see if you were a bird flying high up in the sky over our house?" "What could happen if…?"

Encourage your child to talk about her feelings. Prepare a set of photos cut from magazines that show people experiencing different emotions – happy, sad, angry, frightened, joyful. Ask her which emotions are shown in the pictures, then ask her to talk about her own feelings. "What happens when you feel scared?" You can also use glove puppets to tell a story that features a range of emotions and invite your child to make their puppet speak. Children often find it easier to express their feelings this way.

"Open-ended questions help develop your child's ability to organize and communicate her thoughts out loud."

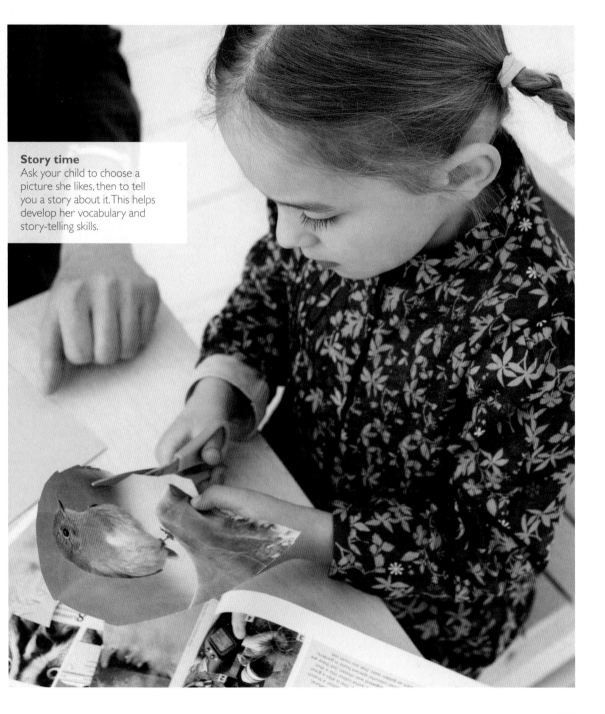

Story time
Ask your child to choose a
picture she likes, then to tell
you a story about it. This helps
develop her vocabulary and
story-telling skills.

the writing road to reading

The process of learning how to read can be as simple as the process of learning how to speak.

In Montessori schools we use a hands-on phonetic approach that helps young children to form a clear understanding of how written words encode the spoken sounds of our language into the symbolic letters of the alphabet. Children learn the sounds made by each letter, and the letter represented by each sound, one letter at a time until they master the entire alphabet. With some basic equipment you can use the same approach at home.

PRESENTING LETTERS

Present letters to your child a few at a time, in these groups:

first set.................c m a t
second set............s r i p
third set.................b f o g
fourth set..............h j u l
fifth set.................d w e n
sixth set.................k q v x y z

Sandpaper letters

These provide a tactile as well as visual way to help children to learn the alphabet. Sandpaper letters are a set of 26 tablets made of painted thin masonite board. On each tablet, a lower case letter has been cut out of fine sandpaper and glued down against a smooth, coloured background. Consonants are printed against pink or red and vowels against blue backgrounds to help children distinguish between them. Sandpaper letters can be bought from a number of suppliers (see page 204) or you can make your own (see box opposite).

As soon as your child shows interest, typically around the age of three, introduce her to a few letters at a time (see box left). Show her how to trace each letter as it would be written, using the middle and index fingers of the hand she normally uses to hold things. As you demonstrate, say the sound that the letter represents in a three-letter phonetic word, such as "cat". The letter "c", for example, represents the sound "kuh".

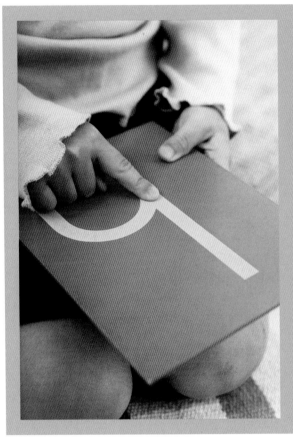

HOW TO MAKE SANDPAPER LETTERS

Use thin masonite board or sturdy cardboard to prepare 26 tablets 20cm (8in) high by 15cm (6in) wide. Some letters, such as "w" may need a wider tablet. Using a non-toxic spray enamel paint, paint each of the tablets. Use blue paint for the tablets for the vowels – a, e, i, o, and u – and pink or red for the tablets for the consonants – b, c, d, f, g, h, j, k, l, m, n, p, q, r, s, t, v, w, x, y, and z.

Next, you need to cut out your letters from fine sandpaper. We have prepared files with the letters made quite large, which you can download from our website (There is a file for lower case letters at http://www.montessori.org/assets/files/405/alphabet_low.pdf and another for capital letters at http://www.montessori.org/assets/files/405/alphabet_caps.pdf). Print them out then use a craft knife to cut out each of the letters to make a stencil that you can then use to cut out your 26 sandpaper letters. Glue each letter down onto a tablet, sandpaper side up and they are ready to use. The next step is to show your child how to trace the sandpaper letters with her finger. Be sure to let her set her own pace.

Sit down beside your child with three sandpaper letters on a small rug. We'll use the letter "c", pronounced "kuh"; the letter "a", pronounced "aah"; and the letter "t", pronounced "tuh". While tracing the letter "c" say: "This is 'kuh'. Can you say 'kuh'?" Most children will say it after you. Now invite your child to trace and sound the letter. As she traces its shape, she is receiving three distinct impressions: the shape of the letter, the feel of its shape and how it is written, and the way you pronounce its sound. Think up words that begin with this sound: "Kuh, cat, can, cap…" This is the first stage of a three-stage lesson (see pages 178–79). Now introduce the second letter, using the same process. Continue on to the second stage of the lesson. "Can you show me 'kuh'? Can you show me 'tuh'?" If your child makes a mistake, present the first stage again and then try the second stage again. "Can you show me 'tuh'? Can you show me 'kuh'?" Now use stages one and two to introduce the third letter "aah". For the third stage of the lesson, lay out the shapes for the letters "c", "a" and "t" before your child and she will pronounce each in turn, "kuh", "aah", "tuh": "cat". She has just read her first word.

Gradually introduce more letters, perhaps two more each week or so, until your child has mastered the entire alphabet. Remember to follow your child. If she becomes bored, end the lesson – your goal is to instill a love of learning and a real interest in reading and composing words, not to produce an early reader at any cost.

Many parents find it curious that in Montessori schools children are not taught the names of the letters, but the sounds that we pronounce as we phonetically sound out words one letter at a time. For a long time, they may not know the names of letters at all, but will call them by the sounds they make "buh", "kuh", "aah", and so on. This eliminates one of the most unnecessary and confusing steps that most children have to go through in learning to read: "A stands for apple. The sound it makes is 'aah'."

It is not uncommon to find that young children who are learning to read this way will be able to compose simple words using prepared alphabet letters several weeks or months before they will be able to read them comfortably. This is a by-product of Montessori's carefully planned introduction to language. Instead of learning words by sight, children spell phonetic words out one sound at a time, which is easier than the process of "decoding" printed words into their component sounds.

Tracing letters in fine sand

A nice extension of the sandpaper letters is to invite your child to trace the letters that she is learning in fine sand, in a tray that is deep enough to minimize accidental spills. After tracing a sandpaper letter on paper, ask her to trace it in the sand. This reinforces her muscle memory of the process of forming the letter and helps her eventual transition into handwriting.

Developing pencil control

Your child needs to develop control of her hand before she can begin to learn to write. Many of the sensorial activities that we have covered in earlier chapters have the extra advantage that they help your child begin to develop the hand–eye coordination so important for handwriting. Give her good-quality coloured pencils to colour in shapes on good-quality paper as a step towards handwriting. Show her how to shade in the shapes carefully using parallel strokes.

A small chalk board and chalk are useful when your child is ready to write. Have her trace one of the sandpaper letters with her fingers, and

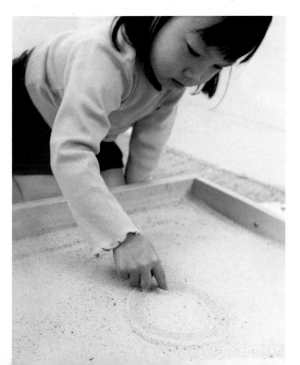

Letters in sand
Once your child has learned to trace letters on paper, she can try tracing them in a tray of sand.

then try to write it on the chalk board. When she can write individual letters, challenge her to begin to compose simple words.

Playing with letters
This game reinforces children's mastery of the sounds of the letters they are learning, as well as helping them to recognize the first sound in any word. To play, you will need to gather small objects whose names begin with the same letter. For example, for the letter "t" you might use a toy train, a truck, and a tractor. Place two or three sandpaper letters on a mat. Place the objects in a basket. Ask your child to select one of the objects and name it. Then ask her, "What sound do you hear at the beginning of the word 'truck'." Pronounce it carefully, sound by sound: "tuh" "rrr" "uhh" "kuh". "Truck begins with 'tuh'. Let's put the truck below the 'tuh' over here." Your child should continue until all of the objects have been placed.

The movable alphabet
Once your child has begun to recognize several letters and their sounds with the sandpaper letters, you can introduce her to a movable alphabet. This is a large box with compartments containing plastic letters, organized much like an old-fashioned printer's box of metal type. You can buy Montessori movable alphabets (see pages 186 and 204) or substitute various other forms of plastic or magnetic letters made for children. Your child can compose words by selecting a small object or picture and then laying out the word for it with the movable letters. As with the sandpaper letters, she sounds out words one letter at a time, selecting the letter that makes the next sound.

YOUR CHILD'S BRAIN
A study comparing Montessori school children with children in other US schools, found that five year olds who had completed the three-year Montessori preschool program scored higher on academic tests than the control group. At age 12, Montessori students wrote more sophisticated and creative stories than children in other programs.

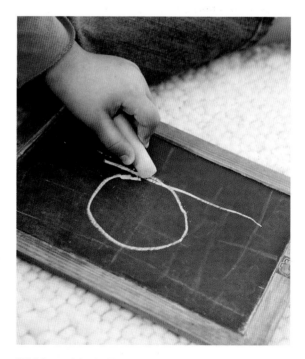

Writing with chalk
A chalk board and chunky piece of chalk are good for practising the letter shapes your child has learned to trace in sand.

Movable alphabet
A large box with 26 compartments
holds sets of letters, which children
use to spell out words.

This phonetic approach has long been recognized by educators as the single most effective way to teach children how to read and write. However, we have to remember that, unlike Italian and Spanish, English is not a completely phonetic language. Just consider the several different sounds made by the letters "ough". There is the sound "off" as in "cough", or "uff" as in "rough" or "enough", or the sound "ohhh" as in the word "though", or the sound "ott" as in "thought". Altogether, there are some 96 different phonograms (combinations of letters that form distinct sounds) in the English language (such as "ph-", "-ee", "ai", "oo", and so on).

As your child begins to compose words, phrases, sentences, and stories, her spelling may sometimes get a bit creative. For example, she may spell the word phone as "fon". Don't worry about correcting her spelling during these early days – it is much better to encourage her to become more confident in her ability to sound words out, rather than risking her losing interest because she gets it wrong.

The process of composing words with the movable alphabet continues for many years, gradually moving from three-letter words to four- and five-letter words with consonant blends ("fl", "tr", "st"), double vowels ("oo", "ee"), silent "e"s and so on.

Starting to read

Typically, there is a smooth transition from reading and writing single words to sentences and stories. For some children this will happen at the age of four; for others when they are five or six. A few will read earlier; others will take a little longer. Remember that all children are different and it is useless to fret if your child isn't as eager as her contemporaries.

No matter how young, as soon as your child shows the slightest interest, begin to teach her how to read. When she is ready, she will pull it all together and will begin to read and write on her own. Use your computer to make cards printed with the names of familiar objects on them. Your child can use these to label all sorts of objects around your home.

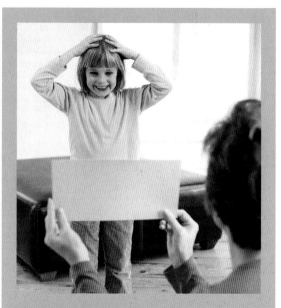

THE VERB GAME

When your child can read whole words, try a more sophisticated version of the command game. Make a set of cards, on each of which is printed a single one-word command (a verb).

Your child picks a card, reads it, then asks you to hold it up while she performs the command: hop, smile, yawn, sleep, clap, sit, stand, wave, eat, drink, put her hands on her head, and so on.

Once she can read one-word command cards, create more advanced card sets using complete sentences: "Bring me a teddy bear" or "Waddle across the room like a duck."

first steps to
mathematics

Teach your child simple maths concepts using games
and hands-on learning materials.

Learning to count by rote is the easiest activity
to build into your daily life. You can count with
your child in many situations: when cooking
together, count how many spoonfuls you need
to add; when out walking, count steps from one
to ten, then start again. A simple game involves
gently tossing a bean bag back and forth between
you and your child, counting every time it's
thrown. Continue to count as high as your child
can manage, then keep going yourself once your
child is no longer certain.

What numbers mean

Grasping the concept of numbers by counting
separate objects is more difficult at first. While
young children can learn to "count" by rote,
reciting the sequence of numbers from one to ten,
most cannot easily grasp the difference between
one quantity and another when looking at more
than three or four objects. It's almost as if they
are thinking: "One, two, three…many!"

One way to avoid this is by allowing children to
visualize the concepts of numbers and quantity
by using a series of segmented rods, rather than
trying to teach them to count sets of separate
objects. In Montessori classrooms, we use a set
of rods that vary in length by 10cm (4in). The
shortest rod is 10cm (4in) long and is painted
red. The second is 20cm (8in) long and is divided
into two 10cm (4in) segments, one red and one
blue. This continues through all 10 rods. You
can buy the Montessori number rods (see page
204) or make your own (see sidebar on page 190).

One of the insights children begin to get
from working with the rods is the nature of
addition and the concept that two numbers
can add to each other. For example, when the
children place the "one" number rod at the
end of the "two" rod, they create a new rod
that is the same length as the "three" rod just
above. They explore similar relationships with
all of the numbers from one to ten.

One, two, three…
The fundamental skill of
counting often crops up
as children play.

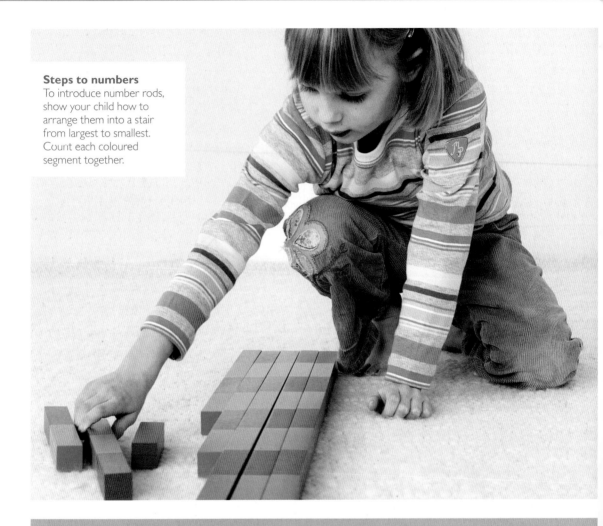

Steps to numbers
To introduce number rods, show your child how to arrange them into a stair from largest to smallest. Count each coloured segment together.

MAKING NUMBER RODS

To make your own set of number rods, use wooden lathe or strip board, approximately the same dimensions as many rulers (5cm/2in wide by about 1cm/½in high). You need to cut or have someone cut 10 lengths: 10cm (4in) long, 20cm (8in), 30cm (12in), up to 100cm (40in). Spray-paint the entire set of strips red. Allow them to dry.

Then, using masking tape, carefully mark off the parts that should be painted blue. For example, the "one"

rod is all red. The "two" rod is red for the first 10cm (4in), then blue for the next 10cm (4in). The "three" rod is red for the first 10cm (4in), blue for the next 10cm (4in), then red again for the last 10cm (4in). This creates alternating lengths of red, blue, red sections. Continue through to the "10" rod, which should be 100cm (40in) in length, painted red, blue, red to form 10 alternating sections.

Counting baskets

These baskets help young children to make the next step in coming to understand the concepts of number and quantity. You need a set of 10 small baskets, each with a card attached labelling the baskets 0, 1, 2, 3, up to 9. You will also need a larger basket containing 45 identical pieces. In Montessori schools we use wooden dowels 1cm (½in) in diameter and 15cm (6in) in length, but at home you could use large wooden beads of the same colour or clothes pegs. Show your child how to count out the correct number of pieces to go in each basket: one, two, three, all the way to nine. Naturally, the basket that is labelled "0" has no pieces, teaching your child at an early age the concept that zero means none (an empty set). If your child counts correctly, she will have no pieces remaining when the last compartment labelled "9" is filled up.

Simple sums

There are all sorts of things you can do with your child around the house to help her practise her skills. Try using dolls to illustrate simple sums. "When Mummy and Daddy first got married there were two of them. Then baby is born. How many are there now?" You can do the same with pieces of fruit, or anything else that comes to hand.

IN PRACTICE Maths in action

Counting almost anything as it occurs during daily life helps your child to understand the quantity that each number represents. Adding and subtracting follow on naturally.

In the basket
As he throws bean bags into a basket, Max calls out the number he gets on target.

Potato counting
Holly practices counting and makes sure everyone in the family gets a potato for dinner.

First maths
Oswin counts oranges in a bowl. His mum removes two and asks "How many are there now?"

exploring science in your home

Your home is an ideal place for scientific experiments that help your child discover how the world works.

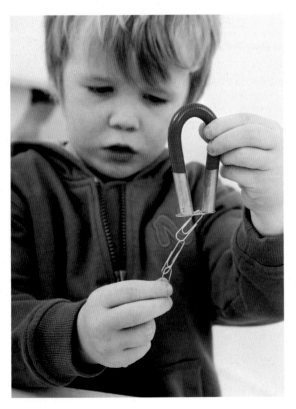

There are so many science activities you can do with your child that I could fill an entire book with them. Many of the activities I have already suggested in this and earlier chapters are science-related: sensory awareness exercises, nature walks, working together in the garden, and the like. Here are just a few more ideas to get your young scientist started.

Magnetic or non-magnetic

Place a number of small objects in a basket, making sure that some of them are made of ferrous material (iron) and can be picked up with a magnet. Prepare two cards, one reading "Magnetic" and the other "Non-magnetic". Ask your child to use a magnet to see which objects it will pick up and which it will not, then place the objects alongside the correct card.

Magical magnetism
Investigating the magnetic properties of different objects is an intriguing activity for young children.

Living or non-living

Fill a basket with toys and small novelty store objects that represent things that are alive (organic) and non-living (inorganic). Prepare cards labelled "Living" and "Non-living". For the objects representing living things you might choose toy birds, forest animals, insects, a tree, and people. For the non-living objects, you might choose objects such as a magnet, a thimble, a toy car, a model house, and a small mirror. Ask your child to set the things that would be living and non-living in the real world alongside the appropriate card.

Sink or float

Gather a number of objects, some of which you know will float and others that will sink. Invite your child to predict which objects will sink and which will float. Set up a basin of water on a tray and place the objects in the water so he can see if he is right.

Sprouting seeds

For this experiment, you will need dried, uncooked butter beans, paper towels, and a plant mister. Show your child how to take a butter bean, place it on a paper towel, wrap it up gently, and then spray the seed and paper towel with water from the plant mister. Remind him to spray the paper towel every day to keep the seed damp. Check for signs that it is starting to sprout. When it does,

Floating fun and games
Your child will love to test out his theories on whether objects will float or sink in a bowl of water.

show your child how to transplant it into a small flowerpot filled with potting soil. Remind him to water it regularly to keep it moist.

A basket of living grass

Take a small basket and fill the bottom with plastic film. Help your child to add 2cm (1in) of small pebbles, then 5cm (2in) of potting soil. Show him how to sprinkle grass seeds over the potting soil and gently press them in. Place the basket on a table next to a window and remind your child to use a plant mister several times a day to keep the seeds damp. In about two weeks he will see the grass seed begin to germinate.

Grow a sock

In autumn, our socks and trousers tend to pick up burrs and other clinging seeds when we go for walks in the woods or through tall grass. Give your child a pair of long sports socks to put on over his trousers. Go for a walk through areas where you are certain to encounter these hitchhiking seeds. When you get home, place the socks in a basin in a place where they will get lots of sun. Soak the socks, leaving one end in the water to continue to soak up more moisture, like a wick. After a week or two, the seeds will begin to germinate and your child will have grown a "living sock".

Exploring roots

Gently dig up a plant with its roots intact. Place it on newspaper and carefully pull the soil away to expose the roots. Explain to your child that every plant uses its roots to absorb water and nutrients from the soil. Repack the soil around the roots and replace the plant in the soil.

Making boats
Use walnut shells, thin card, toothpicks, and modelling clay to make boats that can be launched on a home-made lake.

Walnut shell boats

Children love playing in water. Use a deep tray filled with water as a little lake on which your children can sail small boats made from walnut shells. To make the boats, open a few walnut shells along the edges, being careful not to damage the half shells. Then show your children how to make a sail from a piece of thin card cut to form either a square or a triangle. They can use a toothpick for the mast and mount the sail by poking the toothpick through the cardboard at the right points so that it can catch a breeze. Put modelling clay in the bottom of the shell

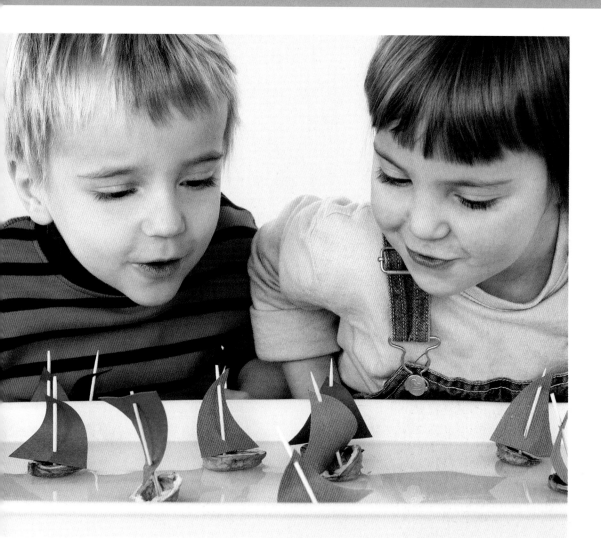

and put the mast into it to hold it upright. Your children are now ready to launch their boats and gently blow to create a breeze.

Pouring air

Young children find it funny that they can make bubbles by submerging a container filled with air underwater and then release (pour) the air by gently tipping the container upwards. This works best in a deep container, such as a bucket, and is even better when the sides of the container are made of glass, as in an aquarium, so everyone can see the bubbles coming up to the surface. Your children can also have fun blowing bubbles under water using straws, especially at bath time.

developing executive functions

A caring family life and an environment rich in activities offer everything a child needs to develop higher-level brain processes.

In essence, the brain's executive functions allow us to plan, organize, and complete tasks. Montessori would not have recognized the term, yet most of her activities are tailor-made for these higher-brain processes. Infants as young as seven months start to exercise these cognitive skills with simple games such as peekaboo or hiding a toy under a blanket. A baby uses working memory as he tracks the hiding places, and exercises inhibitory control as he waits for someone or something to pop back into view. Working memory and impulse control are both at work when he wriggles with excitement as an action song like "Round and round the garden" builds to a predictable climax.

As toddlers turn into preschoolers, matching and sorting games, memory games, and puzzles are great exercise for visual working memory. Children become more flexible in their thinking and can pay attention to different demands in games such as "Follow my leader" and "Simon says". Imaginary play enhances planning skills and self-regulation, especially if children are asked to organize the setting and decide who is going to be mum, dad, or the doctor before they start. When you cook with your children, they develop the ability to wait for instructions, keep tasks in working memory, and pay careful attention to measuring and weighing ingredients.

YOUR CHILD'S
BRAIN

The brain's executive functions begin to develop in infancy. Over time, children become able to focus attention, control their impulses (inhibitory control), and use working memory – the facility to hold and manipulate short-term information in the brain. Working together, executive functions underpin learning, and enable planning and problem-solving.

Half each
Problem-solving can be as simple as finding a way to share when there is only one muffin.

From the age of four or five, board games in which children have to wait their turn, follow a rule, and, later on, involve strategy, use a trio of executive functions – working memory, flexibility, and self-control. Puzzle and brain teaser books exercise attention and problem-solving skills. "I-spy" and "20 questions" are good logic and reasoning games.

Problem-solving

As children grow, parents can help develop their problem-solving capabilities by presenting them with small tasks that encourage them to consider situations, plan, and come up with solutions.

Finding a solution to a problem involves a set of distinct steps: identify the problem; look at the factors that make up the problem; use what you know, your skills, and what you have available to develop a solution; then decide if it worked. Adults have a range of strategies and blueprints based on previous experience that speed up our problem-solving. Children also develop strategies over time, but in the early years, life is rich in novelty, which makes planning and finding solutions especially rewarding. Try the following with your child.

• Before a holiday or trip, give her a small suitcase, ask her to plan what she needs, and let her pack things such as a toothbrush, pyjamas, and cuddly toy.

• At a family meeting (see page 117), ask your wise child to consider a problem and offer advice.

• Before a play or puppet show, get the children to organize props and plan who is doing what.

• Invite your child to solve an everyday dilemma: "Our baby hates being in the supermarket trolley. How can we make it fun for him?"

is Montessori right
for your child?

If you have enjoyed using the ideas in this book, you may want to consider a Montessori school for continuing your child's education.

One of the strengths of Montessori is the atmosphere of cooperation and respect, as different children find joy in learning. Usually, the method is "right" for a wide spectrum of personalities, temperaments, and learning styles. It works for families with a range of learning expectations and, in most cases, parents and teachers work together between home and school to help children learn and develop.

The programme is carefully structured to provide optimal learning opportunities for children. However, parents who are particularly concerned about high achievement may find the Montessori approach difficult to understand and support because it represents an alternative way from the more conventional thinking found in most schools. The belief is that children are born intelligent,

Dance for joy
Montessori schools make learning a fun, joyful, and exciting experience within a caring, organized environment.

curious, and creative, and that all too often schools (and some parents) make the process of learning stressful rather than natural. Families who are generally rather chaotic and disorganized (arrive late in the morning, pick up children at varying times, and find it difficult to attend meetings and work closely with a school) may find a Montessori experience frustrating, although the children from such families often find its structure very reassuring.

Choosing a school

Although most schools try to remain faithful to their understanding of Maria Montessori's insights and research, they have all been influenced by the evolution of our culture and technology over the 100 years since the first Montessori schools were developed. What is more, although the name Montessori refers to a method and philosophy, it is not protected by copyright nor a central licensing or franchising programme. What this means is that, in many parts of the world, anyone could, in theory, open a school and call it Montessori with no knowledge of how an authentic programme is run.

When this happens it is disturbing and embarrassing for those of us who know the difference. Many of these schools fail but often not before they harm the public's perception of Montessori as a whole.

One sign of a school's commitment to excellence is its membership in one of the professional Montessori organizations (see page 204) that offer schools the opportunity to become accredited as well. There are many other smaller Montessori organizations, too, but there is no requirement that a Montessori school be affiliated or accredited by any outside organization. Quite a few Montessori schools choose to remain independent.

No single educational approach will be right for all children. Ideally, parents should seek out the best fit, not only between their child and a particular school, but also between their family's values and goals for their children's education and what given schools realistically offer. Finding the right school for parents is as important as finding the right school for a child. There must be a partnership between them based on the mutual sense that each is a good match for the other.

THE MONTESSORI WAY

Parents who are comfortable with Montessori tend to agree with the following basic ideas about children's learning.

• Intelligence is not rare among human beings. It is found in children at birth. With the right stimulation, the development of reasoning and problem-solving skills can be nurtured in young children.

• The most important years of a child's education are the first six years of life.

• Children should be encouraged to develop a high degree of independence and autonomy.

• Academic competition and accountability are not effective ways to motivate students to become well educated. They learn more effectively when school is seen as a safe, exciting, and joyful experience.

• There is a direct link between children's sense of self-worth, empowerment, and self-mastery, and their ability to learn and retain new skills and information.

• Children learn best through hands-on experience, real-world application, and problem solving rather than through rote learning and testing.

What to look for

In determining which school is the best match for all concerned, you need to trust your eyes, ears, and gut instincts. Nothing beats your own observation and experience. As tempting as it is to enroll your child in a school without entering a classroom, put a visit at the top of your "to do" list. You will learn a great deal by spending 30 minutes to an hour watching the children at work. Ask permission to watch a "work period" first. If you have time, stay for a group meeting or come back later to watch this part of the children's day. The following pointers will help you to know what to look for.

• You should not find rows of desks in a Montessori classroom. There will be no teacher's desk and chalk board in the front of the room. The environment will be set up to make it easy for children to talk to each other and work together. The furniture in the classroom will be the right size for the students.

• Classrooms should be bright, warm, and inviting, filled with plants, animals, art, music, and

Enjoying books
Books are at the heart of every Montessori school. Children progress from picture stories to learning to read at their own pace when they are ready.

books. Interest centres will be filled with intriguing learning materials, mathematical models, maps, charts, international and historical artefacts, a class library, an art area, a small natural science museum, and animals that the children are raising. In a junior school class, you will also find computers and scientific apparatus.

• Classrooms will be organized into several curriculum areas, usually including: language arts (reading, literature, grammar, creative writing, spelling, and handwriting); mathematics and geometry; everyday living skills; sensory awareness exercises and puzzles; geography, history, science, art, music, and movement. Each area will be made up of one or more shelf units, cabinets, and display tables with a wide variety of materials on open display, ready for use as the children select them.

YOUR CHILD'S
BRAIN

Neuroscientific research confirms that a child's first six years last a lifetime. A child comes into the world primed to learn, and the best learning happens in supportive, nurturing relationships, in environments rich in language opportunities, and through children being engaged and active as they develop.

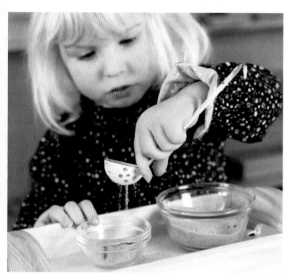

Skilful handling
Practice in everyday skills, such as spooning, helps children to develop hand–eye coordination and fosters competence and independence.

Nice manners
Grace and courtesy are on the curriculum. Montessori children are renowned and respected for their polite behaviour and kindness.

• Each class should contain the full complement of Montessori materials appropriate for that level.
• There will be few if any toys in a Montessori preschool classroom. Instead, there will be an extensive collection of learning materials that match the developmental capabilities, interests, and needs of the children enrolled in each class. These allow for multiple methods of learning and discovery, offering a wide range of intellectual challenges.
• Each class should be led by a Montessori-certified teacher who holds a recognized Montessori credential for the age level taught. Each class would usually include either a second certified Montessori teacher or a trained teacher's assistant. You can expect to find teachers working with one or two children at a time, presenting a new lesson, advising, or quietly observing the class at work.

• A Montessori programme is composed of mixed age groups of children within each classroom, traditionally covering a three-year span from the early childhood level onwards. Ideally, a Montessori class is balanced in terms of boys and girls as well as in the number of children in each age group. Classes should be made up of 25 to 30 children, although these numbers will be lower at the baby and toddler levels.
• Students will usually be found scattered around the classroom, working alone or with one or two others.
• It should be clear that the children feel contented, comfortable, and safe.
If you visit a school and find yourself in love with the look and feel of it and if you can clearly see your child happy and successful in that atmosphere, then that school is likely to be a good fit.

find an activity

This quick guide gives approximate starting ages for ideas and activities. Always be guided by your child's individual development and interests.

Baby sensory exercises (from birth)

Basket of treasures (from 6 months)

Forest walks (from 12 months)

from birth
Baby massage **p.26**
Planning a first bedroom **p.36**
Baby sensory
    exercises **pp.54-57**
Memory box **p.170**

from 6 months
Basket of treasures **p.58**
Reading aloud **p.174**
Keep talking **p.175**
Peekaboo **p.196**
Hide a toy **p.196**
Action rhymes **p.196**

from 12 months
Planning a toddler
    bedroom **p.38**
Walking in the
    woods **p.154**
Ways to introduce new
    vocabulary **p.176**

from 18 months
Stacking bricks **p.64**
Playing with lima beans **p.69**
Listening to music **p.71**
Toilet training **p.93**
Getting dressed **p.96**
Exploring outdoors **p.146**

from two years
Sorting objects **p.64**
Shape stackers **p.66**
Simple puzzles **p.66**
The silence game **p.70**
Herb scents **p.74**
Tidying up **p.84**
Bathroom skills **p.88**
Button frame **p.96**
Putting on a coat **p.98**
Exploring nature **pp.147-8**
Gardening **p.150**
Pet care **p.153**

Getting dressed (from 18 months)

The silence game (from two years)

Make a nature museum (from three years)

Chalkboard (from four years)

index

a

b

c

d

e

f

Penguin
Random
House

Revised Edition
Senior Editor Esther Ripley
Project Art Editor Saffron Stocker
Photographer Ruth Jenkinson
Cover Design Steven Marsden
Pre-Production Producer Robert Dunn
Senior Producer Luca Bazzoli
Managing Editor Dawn Henderson
Managing Art Editor Marianne Markham
Art Director Maxine Pedliham
Publishing Director Mary-Clare Jerram

DK India
Project Editor Janashree Singha
Editor Sugandh Juneja
Senior Art Editor Ira Sharma
Managing Editor Soma B. Chowdhury
Managing Art Editors Navidita Thapa,
    Arunesh Talapatra
Pre-Production Manager Sunil Sharma
DTP Designers Anurag Trivedi,
    Umesh Singh Rawat

First Edition
Senior Editor Esther Ripley
Senior Art Editor Glenda Fisher
Project Art Editor Sara Kimmins
Project Editor Angela Baynham
Designer Hannah Moore
US Editor Jennifer Williams
Photographer Vanessa Davies
DTP Designer Sonia Charbonnier
Production Controller Mandy Inness
Managing Editor Penny Warren
Managing Art Editor Marianne Markham
Picture Researcher Carlo Ortu
Jacket Designer Glenda Fisher
Jacket Editor Adam Powley
Publishing Director Corinne Roberts

The ideas used in this book are based on the author's experience as a Montessori teacher and parent and on the lives and experiences of the many families he has been associated with. While Montessori's methods have been used successfully in school and at home with generations of children, readers should use their own good judgment in deciding which to adopt in their own family. Neither the author nor the publisher shall be liable or responsible for any loss or damage allegedly arising from any information or suggestion in this book.

This edition published in Great Britain in 2017 by
Dorling Kindersley Limited, 80 Strand, London WC2R 0RL

First edition published in Great Britain in 2007

Copyright © 2007, 2017 Dorling Kindersley Limited

A Penguin Random House company
Text copyright © 2007, 2017 Tim Seldin
2 4 6 8 10 9 7 5 3 1
001–299209–June/2017

All rights reserved. No part of this publication may be reproduced, stored in, or introduced into a retrieval system, or transmitted, in any form, or by any means (electronic, mechanical, photocopying, recording, or otherwise), without the prior written permission of the copyright owner.

A CIP catalogue record for this book is available
from the British Library

ISBN 978-0-2412-8626-5

Printed and bound in China

A WORLD OF IDEAS:
SEE ALL THERE IS TO KNOW

www.dk.com

websites and resources

Montessori organizations

Montessori Society AMI UK
montessorisociety.org.uk
Teacher training and list of accredited schools.

Montessori Centre International (MCI)
mci.montessori.org.uk
Teacher training college.

Montessori Education (UK)
montessorieducationuk.org
Umbrella organization listing accredited schools.

Montessori St Nicholas Charity
montessori.org.uk
Charity with magazine for parents.

The Montessori Foundation
montessori.org
Non-profit educational organization that supports the development of Montessori schools around the world. Publishes a parents' journal.

Your child's brain references

p.26 Perry, B (2000) 'Principles of neurodevelopment: an overview': a ChildTrauma Academy Presentation Series 1; No. 2, www.ChildTrauma.org.

p.86 Coldwell J, Pike A, Dunn J (2006) 'Household chaos – links with parenting and child behaviour': *Journal of Child Psychology and Psychiatry*, Nov 2006.

p.113 Piotrowski JT, Lapierre MA, Linebarger DL (2012) 'Investigating correlates of self-regulation in early childhood with a representative sample of English-speaking American families': *Journal of Child and Family Studies*, Apr 2013; 22(3): 423–436.

p.122 Wilhelm I, Rose M, Imhof K I, Rasch B, Beeches C, Born J (2013) 'The sleeping child outplays the adult's capacity to convert implicit into explicit knowledge': *Nature Neuroscience*, 2013, 16, 391–393.

p.145 The Dunedin Multidisciplinary Health and Development Study (DMHDS) – an ongoing, longitudinal study of 1037 New Zealanders from birth in the years 1972–73.

p.149 Wells, N M, Lekies, K S, (2006). 'Nature and the life course: pathways from childhood nature experiences to adult environmentalism': *Children, Youth and Environments,* 16 (1), 41663.

p.177 Biemiller, A (2003) 'Vocabulary needed if children are to read well': *Reading Psychology* 24 (3–4): 323–335.

p.185 Lillard, A S & Else-Quest, N (2006) 'Evaluating Montessori education': *Science* Vol 313, Sept 2006.

acknowledgments

Author's acknowledgments

The book owes a great debt to five of the finest Montessori educators I have ever met: Susan Stephenson, author of *The Joyful Child* and *Child of The World*, co-founder of The Michael Olaf Company in Modesto, California; Susan Tracy, who prepares adults to work with Montessori's youngest students near Chicago, Illinois; K.T. Korngold, former Montessori child, Montessori mom, and gifted writer, who lives in Connecticut; and Jan Katzen-Luchenta and Terri Sherrill, two gifted Montessori educators, writers, and consultants who live respectively in Phoenix, Arizona, and Orlando, Florida. Their ideas continue to reinforce my own and lead me to expand my understanding beyond my own experience. Finally, I would like to thank the fabulous team of editors and designers from Dorling Kindersley in London, and the photographers who bring the book to life.

Publisher's acknowledgments

The publisher would like to thank Emma Forge and Nicola Rodway for original design, Ann Baggaley and Nikki Sims for proof-reading, and Sue Bosanko for the index. Thanks also to Jacqui at Artful Dodgers for the loan of Montessori equipment, to Anna at Sugar Bag Blue for props, and to Kevin Smith, Julianne Boag, Tor Godfrey, and Sarah Webley for photo shoot assistance. Models: Chantal and Eden Richards, Danielle Rampton, Tom Offer, Sonny and Leon Halpenny, Lucius Waterman, Arianna Bellencin, Alessia Burke, Vanessa and Martha Coleman, Jessie and Cherry Eckel, Joanna and Imogen Key, Ben Houchen, Kevin Smith, Isabella and Alexander Moore-Smith, Amilia Rogers, Max Chidwick, Scarlett Sinclair, Joe Williams, Jessica Dopp, Max Newman-Turner, Findlay O'Brian, Poppy, Arthur and Delena McConnell Hunt, Sara, Andy and Lucy Kimmins, Jamie and Joseph Whiteaker, Esther and Sam duSalitoy, Julia, Chris, Rebecca and James Halford, Natalie and Holly Trumper, Amba and Ella Ritchie, Sian Munroe, John and Catherine McFarlane, Tania, William and Ella Stubbs, Alena Daley, Carol and Georgia Armstrong, Keisten Ralph, Marcia, Gemma and Will Gurney-Champion, Michael and Tom Noble, Sarah Webley, Mia and Amelie Nias, Madeline Banner, Heather Lewis, Oswin Moody, Matilda McCarthy, Rose Moss, Poppy and Lily Miller, Tor Godfrey, Anna and Fred Fordham, Julianne Boag, Isaac Gardner, Luc Drew, Emily Smith, Lily-Rose Spick, Sean O'Brien, Ella deVilliers, Emily Butcher, Catriona Roony, Darcy Zander, Freya Morrison, Anna Fitzgerald, Claudia Hurley, Ben Garard, James Chiradani, Patrick Willson, Maxim Georgiou, Will Harris, Vishaka Thakrar, Toby Droy, Rocio Chacon, Lucy Hawkins, Zoe Glasier, Sarah Bridgman, Helen Hatswell, Florence Hatswell, Louise Onikoyi, Freddie Allison, April Morgan, Flora Morgan, Alex Ng, Elizabeth Fox, Rose Lally, Maria Lally, Arthur Fox, Ollie Barnett, Georgia Barnett, Frazer Blaxland, Dawn Henderson, and John Hughes.

Picture credits

Dorling Kindersley would like to thank the following for their kind permission to reproduce their photographs: 13 Library of Congress, Washington, D.C.: Harris & Ewing (br)
All other images © Dorling Kindersley Limited
For further information see: www.dkimages.com